Introduction

Building a foundation for writing begins with strategies and creative ideas. *Weekly Writing Lessons* gives the young author ideas and strategies for writing stories with strong introductions, transitions, conclusions, elaboration, and literary devices. Each strategy is introduced and developed over a period of five days. The lessons build on one another, culminating in a series of five writing projects that incorporate all strategies learned.

The format begins with direct instruction on the first day that introduces the student to the strategy. The teacher continues to model the strategy with the class on the next day. On the third day, students work with partners to delve into the writing concepts using various skills and techniques in a fun way. The fourth day provides the student with an independent writing assignment that includes instructional guidance. The five-day lesson ends with a writing assignment that the student completes independently. This plan can be used as a Monday through Friday activity, or teachers can begin the plan on any day and continue for five days. Students who are proficient writers, as well as those who find it difficult to get started with a writing assignment, will benefit from this five-day plan.

Five-Day Lesson Planner

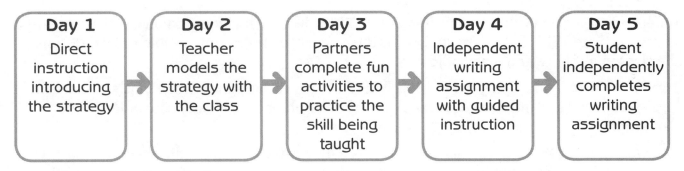

Day 1	Day 2	Day 3	Day 4	Day 5
Direct instruction introducing the strategy	Teacher models the strategy with the class	Partners complete fun activities to practice the skill being taught	Independent writing assignment with guided instruction	Student independently completes writing assignment

Additionally, *Weekly Writing Lessons* is a one-step resource for the teacher, providing complete five-day plans for developing writing strategies from the opening to the closing and in between. This comprehensive workbook eliminates the teacher's continual search for instructional writing materials. It was developed to meet the needs of both the teacher and the student.

Weekly Writing Lessons prepares students to communicate ideas in any writing format. The workbook is an essential resource to help students in grades five through six to meet the demands of today's standardized testing. More importantly, *Weekly Writing Lessons* teaches children valuable writing skills that will be used throughout their lives.

How to Use the Book

Weekly Writing Lessons is a writer's workbook for the young author, as well as a complete five-day planner for the busy teacher. The workbook consists of five chapters, each containing lessons on a particular concept of writing. Each lesson is taught over the course of five days of instruction. The workbook is comprehensive and easy to follow for both teacher and student. The chapters can be taught sequentially, or in the order that best meets the needs of the students.

Each lesson in *Weekly Writing Lessons* begins with teacher instruction. On **day one**, the teacher will introduce the lesson with a short explanation of what will be taught, an example of usage, and a list of vocabulary or phrases that will be used in the lesson. The teacher should preview the list with the class so the students understand the words or phrases that will be used in the lesson. The teacher will then guide the whole class in activities related to the strategy.

The teacher will model the writing skill on **day two**. A class paragraph will be created with the teacher. The instructor can display the paragraph during the teaching of the five-day lesson. The children can keep their copies in notebooks or binders to use as a reference for future stories.

Day three of each lesson is a partner activity. This activity can also be completed in small groups depending on the size and demands of the class. The activity uses the skill being taught in a fun and interesting way.

Independent writing will begin on **day four**. These lessons include guidance and a structured writing activity. This is an opportunity for the teacher to observe any problems or questions the class might have and make adjustments.

Day five has students using the writing skill to write a paragraph independently. They will be given story ideas and a list of vocabulary words or phrases that can be included in the paragraph.

Weekly Writing Lessons provides the students with strategies that can be used to write any story. It includes a format for planning what will be written, as well as ample opportunities for practice. The students will check their work at the end of the lesson and make revisions. There are many opportunities for the students to share what they have written with the teacher and class. The teacher will be able to use this sharing as formative assessment and adjust the instruction accordingly.

At the end of the book, there is a writing assessment. The students will use all the writing concepts taught to write five complete stories. A writing checklist is included to allow the student to check off the concepts that were used. Each story will take several days to complete, ending with a finished copy for the teacher to assess.

Each student's writing should be kept in a notebook or binder, or on a computer, if available. While space for writing is provided on individual worksheets wherever possible, students may need to write or finish activities on seperate paper. Throughout *Weekly Writing Lessons*, students are writing paragraphs that address a particular skill. These paragraphs can be used to inspire a complete story. In addition to these writing opportunities, a Story Ideas page is included at the end of the workbook to give the teacher and students numerous writing ideas.

Weekly Writing Lessons provides a resource for day-to-day writing lessons and equips young authors with skills and strategies to make them successful writers.

Editor
Amethyst W. Gaidelis, M.A.

Editor in Chief
Ina Massler Levin, M.A.

Creative Director
Karen J. Goldfluss, M.S. Ed.

Cover Artist
Barb Lorseyedi

Art Coordinator
Renée Mc Elwee

Imaging
Ariyanna Simien

GRADES 5-6

WEEKLY WRITING LESSONS

- teaches vital writing strategies
- organized by the week for easy use
- scaffolded to build writing independence
- incorporates formative and summative assessments
- whole-group, partner, and independent activities

Teacher Created Resources

Publisher
Mary D. Smith, M.S. Ed.

Authors
Sandra Cook, M.A. & Helen Leon, M.A.

Teacher Created Resources
6421 Industry Way
Westminster, CA 92683
www.teachercreated.com

ISBN: 978-1-4206-2635-3

©2013 Teacher Created Resources
Made in U.S.A.

Teacher Created Resources

Table of Contents

Common Core Standards

The activities in this book are correlated to the Common Core State Standards © Copyright 2010. National Governors Association Center for Best Practices and Council of Chief State School Officers. All rights reserved. For more information about the Common Core State Standards, go to *http://www.corestandards.org/*.

Grade 5 Writing	
Text Types and Purposes	
Standard 3: W.5.3	Write narratives to develop real or imagined experiences or events using effective technique, descriptive details, and clear event sequences.
W.5.3a	Orient the reader by establishing a situation and introducing a narrator and/or characters; organize an event sequence that unfolds naturally.
W.5.3b	Use narrative techniques, such as dialogue, description, and pacing, to develop experiences and events or show the responses of characters to situations.
W.5.3c	Use a variety of transitional words, phrases, and clauses to manage the sequence of events.
W.5.3d	Use concrete words and phrases and sensory details to convey experiences and events precisely.
W.5.3e	Provide a conclusion that follows from the narrated experiences or events.
Production and Distribution of Writing	
Standard 5: W.5.5	With guidance and support from peers and adults, develop and strengthen writing as needed by planning, revising, editing, rewriting, or trying a new approach.
Range of Writing	
Standard 10: W.5.10	Write routinely over extended time frames and shorter time frames for a range of discipline-specific tasks, purposes, and audiences.
Grade 5 Language	
Vocabulary Acquisition and Use	
Standard 5: L.5.5	Demonstrate understanding of figurative language, word relationships, and nuances in word meanings.

Grade 6 Writing	
Text Types and Purposes	
Standard 3: W.6.3	Write narratives to develop real or imagined experiences or events using effective technique, relevant descriptive details, and well-structured event sequences.
W.6.3a	Engage and orient the reader by establishing a context and introducing a narrator and/or characters; organize an event sequence that unfolds naturally and logically.
W.6.3b	Use narrative techniques, such as dialogue, pacing, and description, to develop experiences, events, and/or characters.
W.6.3c	Use a variety of transition words, phrases, and clauses to convey sequence and signal shifts from one time frame or setting to another.
W.6.3d	Use precise words and phrases, relevant descriptive details, and sensory language to convey experiences and events.
W.6.3e	Provide a conclusion that follows from the narrated experiences or events.
Production and Distribution of Writing	
Standard 5: W.6.5	With some guidance and support from peers and adults, develop and strengthen writing as needed by planning, revising, editing, rewriting, or trying a new approach.
Range of Writing	
Standard 10: W.6.10	Write routinely over extended time frames and shorter time frames for a range of discipline-specific tasks, purposes, and audiences.
Grade 6 Language	
Vocabulary Acquisition and Use	
Standard 5: L.6.5	Demonstrate understanding of figurative language, word relationships, and nuances in word meanings.

Begin a Story with Onomatopoeia

Writers often open stories by using onomatopoeia. Onomatopoeia is a word that imitates the sound it represents. It is often called a sound word because it captures special sounds. The writer can also include onomatopoetic words throughout the story to help the reader visualize what is happening.

Example: ***Thump, thump, thump!*** *I heard the heavy footsteps coming up the creaky stairs. I knew no one was home, yet the sound was unmistakable. Someone was in my house! Who could it be? What should I do?*

Onomatopoetic Words

crackle	sizzle	gurgle	whoosh	growl	zoom	rustle	screech
slurp	jingle	zap	thud	fizz	snort	poof	rattle

Whole Group As a class, let's fill in the blanks with the onomatopoetic words that make the best Outstanding Openers for each story opener.

1. _____ ! The tires squealed as the car sped away.

2. _____ ! My stomach would not stop making noises.

3. _____ ! Nicholas flew by on his skateboard.

4. _____ ! The coconut fell from the tree.

5. _____ ! Mom is making bacon.

Independently Now work independently to list four different onomatopoetic words. Use any onomatopoetic word of your choice or find a word from the box. Don't choose an onomatopoetic word that has been used before.

1. _____   3. _____

2. _____   4. _____

Write a sentence using each of the above words.

1. _____

2. _____

3. _____

4. _____

Whole Group Share your favorite sentence with the class.

Begin a Story with Onomatopoeia

An onomatopoetic word is a word that imitates the sound it represents. Onomatopoetic words at the beginning of a story will grab the reader's attention. A writer can include onomatopoetic words throughout the story to help the reader visualize what is happening.

Whole Group Let's write an opening paragraph using "growl" as our onomatopoetic word.

Brainstorming Time!

A. As a class, list things that make a "growl" sound.

1. _____   3. _____

2. _____   4. _____

B. Next, help think of opening sentences for two of the topics above.

1. **Growl!** _____

2. **Growl!** _____

Independently Select one of these sentences as the beginning for a paragraph. Write a paragraph using "growl" as your onomatopoetic word, and begin with the sentence you chose. Your sound must always make sense with the topic you are writing about. Remember, you can use onomatopoetic words throughout the story.

Growl! _____

_____

_____

_____

_____

_____

_____

Check Your Work

Do the sound words make your story come alive?

Circle all the onomatopoetic words you included in the paragraph.

How many did you use?

Whole Group Share your paragraph with the class.

Begin a Story with Onomatopoeia

An onomatopoetic word is a word that imitates the sound it represents. Onomatopoetic words at the beginning of a story will grab the reader's attention and will help bring the story to life.

Onomatopoetic Words

click	whoosh	bang	whizz	screech	ding	ahhh	rumble
clack	boing	clang	thud	squeak	crash	zoom	kurplunk

Partners Read the paragraph. Working with a partner, choose a word from the list to fill in each blank. Endings such as *-ed, -ing,* or *-s* can be added to the sound words if necessary.

(1) _____ ! The roller coaster has arrived. I jumped in and, (2) _____, the bar came down. (3) _____ , (4)_____, the wheels went as we climbed to the top. (5) _____ ! Everyone was screaming as the roller coaster (6) _____ down the hill. (7)_____ ! The coaster was heading for the last loop. Suddenly we were upside down and then we were going sideways. (8)_____ ! I was thrown into the person next to me. Thankfully, the roller coaster (9)_____ to a halt. Hurray! I survived!

Independently Now, independently find alternative onomatopoetic words for the paragraph. Each blank should be different from the one you completed with your partner.

(1) _____ ! The roller coaster has arrived. I jumped in and (2) _____ the bar came down. (3) _____ ! (4) _____ ! The wheels went as we climbed to the top. (5) _____ ! Everyone was screaming as the roller coaster (6) _____ down the hill. (7) _____ ! The coaster was heading for the last loop. Suddenly we were upside down and then we were going sideways. (8) _____ ! I was thrown into the person next to me. Thankfully, the roller coaster (9) _____ to a halt. Hurray! I survived!

Check Your Work

Do the onomatopoetic words make sense in the paragraph?

Do the sound words add exciting details to the paragraph?

Which paragraph do you like better? Why?

Whole Group Share one paragraph with the class.

Begin a Story with Onomatopoeia

An onomatopoetic word is a word that imitates the sound it represents. Onomatopoetic words at the beginning of a story will grab the reader's attention. A writer can include onomatopoetic words throughout the story to help the reader visualize what is happening.

Brainstorming Time!

Whole Group As a class, use the opening onomatopoetic word "hiss" to think of sentences about the following things.

1. snake: **Hiss!** _____

2. bottle: **Hiss!** _____

3. tires: **Hiss!** _____

4. vampire: **Hiss!** _____

Independently Write an opening paragraph using the word "hiss." Select one of the above sentences to begin the paragraph. Write the opening paragraph with the topic sentence you selected. The sound must always make sense with the topic you are writing about.

Hiss! _____

_____

_____

_____

_____

_____

_____

_____

Check Your Work

Does the onomatopoetic word make sense with the topic?

Did you use onomatopoetic words throughout the paragraph?

Whole Group Share your paragraph with the class.

Begin a Story with Onomatopoeia

An onomatopoetic word is a word that imitates the sound it represents. Onomatopoetic words at the beginning of a story will grab the reader's attention. These words can also be included throughout the story to help the reader visualize what is happening.

Independently Write an opening paragraph using any onomatopoetic word of your choice or find a word from the list below.

Onomatopoetic Words

crackle	sizzle	gurgle	whoosh	growl	zoom	rustle	screech
slurp	jingle	zap	thud	fizz	snort	poof	rattle

A. What onomatopoetic word did you choose? Why?

I chose the word _____ because _____ .

Brainstorming Time!

B. List things that make the sound of the onomatopoetic word you chose.

1. _____   3. _____

2. _____   4. _____

C. Write opening sentences for two of the topics you listed above.

1. _____

2. _____

Select one of these sentences for your opening paragraph.

D. Write an opening paragraph about your topic using the onomatopoetic word you chose. Remember that onomatopoetic words can be used throughout your paragraph to paint a vivid picture for the reader.

_____

_____

_____

_____

Check Your Work

Did you remember to use onomatopoetic words throughout the paragraph?

Whole Group Share your paragraph with the class.

Begin a Story with an Interrogative Sentence

A good writer looks for interesting ways to begin a story. An interrogative sentence asks a question. Asking a question is a great way to grab the reader's attention and spark the reader's curiosity.

Example: *Why is everyone screaming? It's only a movie. Werewolves aren't real. That is what Devin thought until he met one face to face.*

Interrogative Words

who	what	where	when	how	which	why	whose
did	do	is	are	can	could	would	should

Whole Group Read the following sentences. These sentences are answers. Can you think of the questions? Write an interrogative sentence for each of the answers.

Example: *I will wear my blue shirt to the party.*   *What should I wear to the party?*

Answer	Question
1. The movie starts at 3 o'clock.	*When does th* _____
2. The book is on the top shelf.	_____
3. Paul was called to the principal's office.	_____

Independently Write interrogative sentences independently.

A. Write an interrogative sentence for each of the answers below. Remember to end the sentence with a question mark.

1. The kitten was meowing at my door. _____

2. Wanda found the article on the Internet. _____

3. Tiffany's mother drove her to the mall. _____

4. The boys met at the park to play baseball. _____

B. Write interrogative sentences to find out what happened at recess. Don't forget a question mark at the end of each sentence.

1. _____

2. _____

3. _____

Whole Group Share your favorite interrogative sentence with the class.

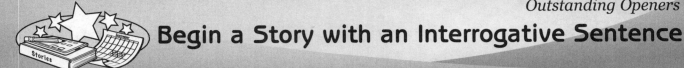

Begin a Story with an Interrogative Sentence

An interrogative sentence asks a question. Asking a question at the beginning of a story grabs the reader's attention and sparks the reader's curiosity.

Interrogative Words

who	what	where	when	how	which	why	whose
did	do	is	are	can	could	would	should

Brainstorming Time!

Whole Group What question could be used to begin this paragraph?

_____ *? Julia could not believe her eyes as she saw her favorite basketball player enter the gym.*

Create a list of interrogative sentences that could be used to fill in the blank.

1. _____

2. _____

3. _____

Independently Now use one of your interrogative sentences as the beginning of a paragraph.

A. Select the interrogative sentence that you want to use as the beginning to your paragraph. Then make a list of events you want to include in your paragraph. The events should be listed in the order in which they will appear in the paragraph.

1. _____   3. _____

2. _____   4. _____

B. Write an opening paragraph using the interrogative sentence you chose and the events you listed.

_____ *? Julia could not believe her eyes when she saw her favorite basketball player enter the gym.* _____

_____

_____

Check Your Work

Does your interrogative sentence grab the reader's attention?

Whole Group Share your paragraph with the class.

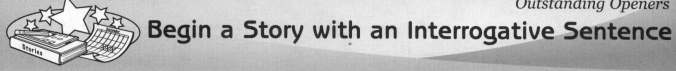

Begin a Story with an Interrogative Sentence

An interrogative sentence asks a question. Asking a question is a great way to grab the reader's attention and spark the reader's curiosity. It is also a good way to obtain information.

Have you ever listened to an interview? An interview is a meeting where information is gathered from a special person. The answers to these questions can be used to write an informational paragraph.

Partners With a partner, interview a fictional character, such as a cartoon character or a super hero.

A. Choose a character together. What fictional character did you choose?

We chose _____ **because** _____ .

B. Write three questions to ask the character, and then write the character's answers. Good interview questions provide the reader with unique details about the character. Do not include questions that can be answered by saying *yes* or *no*.

Example

Unsatisfactory: *Do you like living in the sea? Yes.*

Satisfactory: *Why do you like living in the sea? I like watching the amazing creatures.*

1. **Question:** _____

   Answer: _____

2. **Question:** _____

   Answer: _____

3. **Question:** _____

   Answer: _____

Independently Using the answers you created, write a paragraph. In the paragraph, put your information together in an interesting way.

_____

_____

_____

_____

Check Your Work

Does the paragraph have interesting facts and details?

Whole Group Share your paragraph with the class.

Begin a Story with an Interrogative Sentence

An interrogative sentence asks a question. Asking a question is a great way to grab the reader's attention and spark the reader's curiosity.

Interrogative Words

who	what	where	when	how	which	why	whose
did	do	is	are	can	could	would	should

Independently Begin a paragraph with an interrogative sentence.

A. Use the following topics to write interrogative sentences that could begin a paragraph. Choose words from the box to begin your opening interrogative sentence.

    1. **a sporting event:** _____

    2. **a disagreement with a friend:** _____

    3. **a dance:** _____

B. Select one of the above openings to begin the paragraph. Which interrogative opener would make the best story starter?

The interrogative sentence that would make the best opener is number _____ *because*

_____ .

C. Make a list of events you want to include in your paragraph. The events should be listed in the order in which they will appear in the paragraph.

    1. _____   3. _____

    2. _____   4. _____

D. Write an opening paragraph with the opener you selected and the events from Part C. Remember to use a question mark at the end of your interrogative sentence.

_____

_____

_____

_____

Check Your Work

Will the interrogative opening sentence spark the interest of the reader?

Did you add details to help the reader understand what is happening next?

Whole Group Share your paragraph with the class.

Begin a Story with an Interrogative Sentence

An interrogative sentence asks something. A writer can begin a story with an interrogative sentence to trigger the reader's interest and curiosity. Starting with a question will have the reader wondering what will happen next.

Interrogative Words

who	what	where	when	how	which	why	whose
did	do	is	are	can	could	would	should

Interrogative Sentences

Where did I leave my book bag?   How can I get all this work done?

Whose jacket is this?   Should I invite Andrew to the party?

Whatever happened to the girl who lived down the street?

Independently Write an opening paragraph using any interrogative sentence of your choice or with a question from the box.

A. Write the interrogative sentence you will use to begin your paragraph.

_____

B. Make a list of events you want to include in your paragraph. The events should be listed in the order in which they will appear in the paragraph.

1. _____   3. _____

2. _____   4. _____

C. Write an opening paragraph beginning with the interrogative sentence from Part A. Make sure you include the events from Part B. Your interrogative opening should have the reader imagining what will happen next.

_____

_____

_____

_____

Check Your Work

Will the interrogative opener have the reader wondering what will happen next?

Whole Group Share your paragraph with the class.

Begin a Story with Dialogue

When a character speaks, his or her exact words are called dialogue. Dialogue lets the reader know what the character is saying and thinking.

Example: *"That's strange," screeched Andrew. "There is a snowman walking across our front yard!"*

In dialogue, a speaker tag tells the reader who is speaking. *Screeched Andrew* is a speaker tag.

Speaker Tags

argued	whispered	screamed	exclaimed	announced
blurted	cried	complained	screeched	yelled
groaned	shouted	explained	gasped	sighed
laughed	declared	replied	answered	repeated

Whole Group Write dialogue for each of the characters. Make sure the character's dialogue makes sense with the speaker tag.

A. In the following exercises, the dialogue will come after the speaker's name.

1. **Wu groaned, "** _____ **."**

2. **Maria gasped, "** _____ **!"**

B. In the next group of exercises, the dialogue will come before the speaker's name.

1. **"** _____ **," Osvaldo explained.**

2. **"** _____ **," laughed Drew.**

C. Divided dialogue is dialogue that is separated by the speaker's name and a speaker tag, such as *Mary replied*. Write divided dialogues on the lines below.

1. **"** _____ **," Pauline sighed. "** _____ **."**

2. **"** _____ **," yelled Claudia. "** _____ **!"**

Independently Write three examples of dialogue. In one, put the dialogue after the speaker's name, like you did in Part A. In another one, put the dialogue before the speaker's name, like in Part B. In a third, write a divided dialogue, like in Part C.

1. _____

2. _____

3. _____

Whole Group Share your favorite dialogue with the class.

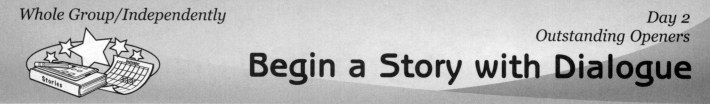

Begin a Story with Dialogue

When a character speaks, his or her exact words are called dialogue. Dialogue lets the reader know what the character is saying and thinking. Dialogue can bring characters to life.

Speaker Tags

argued	whispered	screamed	exclaimed	announced
blurted	cried	complained	screeched	yelled
groaned	shouted	explained	gasped	sighed
laughed	declared	replied	answered	repeated

Brainstorming Time!

Whole Group Write dialogue that someone might say about the opening day for the fastest roller coaster in the amusement park. You can use a divided dialogue, or the dialogue can come before or after the speaker tag.

1. _____

2. _____

3. _____

Independently Let's write an opening paragraph using dialogue as our Outstanding Opener.

A. Circle the dialogue above you think would make the best opener for the paragraph.

B. Think about a time you rode on a roller coaster. Make a list of events you will include in the paragraph.

1. _____   3. _____

2. _____   4. _____

C. Write the opening paragraph. Remember, you can use a divided dialogue, or the dialogue can come before or after the speaker tag.

_____

_____

_____

_____

Check Your Work

Does the dialogue make sense with the character's actions?

Whole Group Share your paragraph with the class.

Begin a Story with Dialogue

Dialogue is a conversation between two or more characters in a story. The characters become more real when the writer uses dialogue. It is important to know that a new paragraph is required every time the speaker changes.

Example

"Where have you been? I was looking for you. Are you okay?" Krystal whispered.

"I'm alright now," Nicole said.

"What happened?" Krystal asked anxiously.

"Somehow I got trapped in the basement. I was there all morning. Luckily, my mom came home for lunch and found me," Nicole explained.

Speaker Tags

argued	whispered	screamed	exclaimed	announced
blurted	cried	complained	screeched	yelled
groaned	shouted	explained	gasped	sighed
laughed	declared	replied	answered	repeated

Partners Working with a partner, write a conversation between two friends using dialogue.

A. Choose one of the ideas below for your conversation and circle it.

Going shopping   A day at the beach

A game   A favorite television program

B. Write the dialogue between two friends using the idea you chose. Remember to start a new paragraph every time a different person is talking.

_____

_____

_____

_____

_____

_____

_____

Check Your Work

Does the dialogue bring the characters to life?

Whole Group Share the conversation with the class.

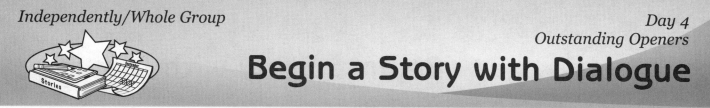

Begin a Story with Dialogue

Dialogue is the exact words that characters are thinking or saying. Writers can start stories with dialogue to spark the interest of the reader.

Speaker Tags

argued	whispered	screamed	exclaimed	announced
blurted	cried	complained	screeched	yelled
groaned	shouted	explained	gasped	sighed
laughed	declared	replied	answered	repeated

Independently How would the following characters express themselves? Write dialogue for each event. Then write your own paragraph.

A. Write one line of dialogue for each of the events below. Remember to place quotation marks before and after what the character is saying.

Example: *Julia lost her sister's video game.* *"She will never forgive me," Julia cried.*

1. The teacher caught Vicky talking. _____

2. Nick's bike had a flat tire. _____

3. Wu spilled grape juice on his new jacket. _____

B. Circle the above dialogue that will make the best opener for your paragraph.

C. Make a list of events you will include in the paragraph. List events in the order in which they happen in the story.

1. _____   3. _____

2. _____   4. _____

D. Write an opening paragraph using the dialogue you chose and the list of events.

_____

_____

_____

_____

_____

Check Your Work

Does the dialogue spark the interest of the reader?

Whole Group Share your paragraph with the class.

Begin a Story with Dialogue

When a character speaks, his or her exact words are called dialogue. Dialogue lets the reader know what the character is saying and thinking. Dialogue can bring the characters to life.

Independently Write an opening paragraph using any dialogue of your choice or from the box.

Dialogue Starters

David declared, "The dog ate my homework!"

"No way!" yelled Mia. "I won't go!"

"Were you invited to the party?" Debbie asked.

"Wait a minute," complained the boy. "I can't find my phone."

Speaker Tags

argued	whispered	screamed	exclaimed	announced
blurted	cried	complained	screeched	yelled
groaned	shouted	explained	gasped	sighed
laughed	declared	replied	answered	repeated

A. Write the dialogue starter you will use in your paragraph.

_____ .

B. Make a list of events you want to include in your paragraph. The events should be listed in the order in which they will appear in the paragraph.

1. _____   3. _____

2. _____   4. _____

C. Write an opening paragraph beginning with the dialogue from Part A. Make sure you include the events from Part B.

_____

_____

_____

_____

_____

Check Your Work

Does the opening dialogue make your character sound believable?

Did you put the quotation marks in the correct places?

Whole Group Share your paragraph with the class.

Begin a Story with a Teaser

Teasers are sentences or paragraphs that give the reader just enough juicy information to create a feeling of suspense and interest. The reader has to read on to find out what happens.

Example: *Samantha was strolling in the park when she looked up and saw a statue wink at her. She looked again, and everything seemed normal. Samantha started to walk away when suddenly the statue winked once more.*

Whole Group As a group, let's practice writing teasers.

A. Fill in the blanks with the teaser from the list that makes the best opener for each paragraph.

> ### Teasers
> I was eating my breakfast when suddenly the house became dark.
> Something was on his pillow.
> He woke up to find himself on a moving train.

1. _____

Matthew had no idea where he was going. He kept looking for something that was familiar, but everything was different.

2. _____

All at once, the table started to shake. Then it began to rise off the floor. It was getting higher and higher.

3. _____

It was furry, warm, and touching his cheek. He was afraid to open his eyes to see what it was.

B. Write an opening teaser for the following paragraph. Make sure it is mysterious and unexpected.

_____

Nicholas was jogging down the road, when a hole suddenly appeared in front of him. He almost fell into it. The hole was getting larger and larger as he watched in amazement.

Independently Write an opening teaser for the following paragraph.

_____

The room was so dark that I could not see a thing. Then I heard a strange sound in front of me. I tried to get away, but the door slammed shut.

Whole Group Share your teaser with the class.

Begin a Story with a Teaser

Teasers are sentences or paragraphs that give the reader just enough juicy information to create a feeling of suspense and interest. Teasers are often mysterious. The reader will have to keep reading to find out what happens.

Whole Group Let's write a teaser about the following situation:

You answered a call on your cell phone, and all you could hear was laughing.

Brainstorming Time!

We will make a list of teasers that could be used in this situation. Think of strange or mysterious openers about just hearing laughing on the phone. The teaser should make the reader wonder what will happen next.

1. _____

2. _____

3. _____

Independently Now complete the paragraph.

A. Select the teaser that you want to use to begin your paragraph, and circle it.

B. Make a list of events to include in the paragraph. The events should be written in the order they will appear in the story.

1. _____ 3. _____

2. _____ 4. _____

C. Use the opening teaser and the list of events from Part B to complete the paragraph. Make the reader wonder what will be revealed as the story unfolds.

_____

_____

_____

_____

Check Your Work

Did the reader wonder what would happen next?

How did you make the paragraph mysterious?

Whole Group Share your paragraph with the class.

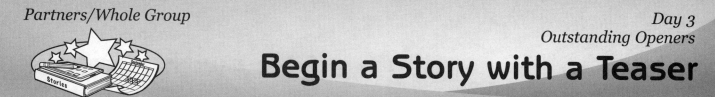

Begin a Story with a Teaser

A mystery is a fictional story that has a puzzle or problem that needs to be solved. It is the job of a detective to discover clues and find the solution. A teaser is a sentence that can mystify and baffle a reader because not all the information is given right away.

Partners   Working with a partner, pretend you are detectives and you are trying to solve a mystery. The title of the mystery is "The Case of the Missing Book."

A. Brainstorm the following information for your paragraph:

Setting — Where does the story take place? _____

When does the story take place? _____

Characters — Name and description: _____

Name and description: _____

Problem — What is the mystery? _____

Clues — What clues were discovered to solve the problem?	**Plot** — List 3 events that will show how each clue was discovered.
1. _____	1. _____
2. _____	2. _____
3. _____	3. _____

Solution — The case was solved when _____ .

B. With your partner, think of two opening teasers for your mystery paragraph.

1. _____

2. _____

C. Select the teaser that you think is the best opener for the paragraph. Then, write an opening paragraph using the teaser from Part B and the information from Part A.

_____

_____

_____

_____

_____

Check Your Work

Did you intrigue and baffle the reader with your teaser?

Whole Group Share your paragraph with the class.

Begin a Story with a Teaser

Teasers are sentences or paragraphs that give the reader just enough juicy information to create a feeling of suspense and interest. Teasers are often mysterious. The reader will have to keep reading to find out what happens.

Independently Write a paragraph using the following situation. Show what happens next or how you begin to solve the mystery.

You wake up and your hair is white.

A. Use the following words to create opening teasers. Think of something strange and mysterious to tease the reader into reading more.

1. **bedroom:** _____

2. **mirror:** _____

3. **shampoo:** _____

4. **hat:** _____

Select one of these teasers for your opening paragraph. Which teaser would create the best story?

The best opening teaser is number _____ because _____ .

B. Make a list of events to include in the paragraph. The events should be written in the order they will appear in the story.

1. _____   3. _____

2. _____   4. _____

C. Write an opening paragraph using the teaser from Part A and the events from Part B. The teaser should have the reader wondering what will happen next in the paragraph.

_____

_____

_____

_____

_____

Check Your Work

Does your paragraph have the reader wondering what strange and mysterious thing will happen next?

Does the teaser make sense with the rest of the paragraph?

Whole Group Share your paragraph with the class.

Begin a Story with a Teaser

Teasers are sentences or paragraphs that give the reader just enough juicy information to create a feeling of suspense and interest. Teasers are often mysterious. Remember, the readers' curiosity will make them want to read on.

Independently Write an opening paragraph using any teaser of your choice or find a teaser from the list below.

> ### Teasers
>
> Mandy arrived at school, but the doors were locked.
>
> The television was blaring, but Debbie couldn't turn it off.
>
> I looked in the mirror and saw someone else's face.
>
> A strange box is in front of my door.
>
> Mary is looking at me with a surprised look on her face.

A. What teaser will you use for your opening paragraph? Why?

I chose _____

because _____.

B. Make a list of events to include in the paragraph. The events should be written in the order they will appear in the story.

1. _____   3. _____

2. _____   4. _____

C. Write an opening paragraph using the teaser you chose and the events from Part B. Make sure the teaser is something strange and mysterious that the reader does not expect. The teaser should spark the reader's curiosity.

_____

_____

_____

_____

> ### Check Your Work
>
> Is the teaser suspenseful?
>
> Does the paragraph describe a mysterious event?

Whole Group Share your paragraph with the class.

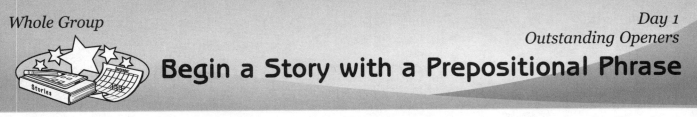

Begin a Story with a Prepositional Phrase

A writer can use prepositional phrases to include important information at the beginning of a story. A prepositional phrase begins with a preposition and ends with a noun or pronoun. Prepositional phrases expand sentences by adding details. They can give many types of information. The prepositional phrases below answer the questions *where* and *when*.

Example: *Throughout my recital, I could hear a low, annoying murmur.*
Was someone trying to distract me so I would make a mistake?

Prepositions

above	during	under	by	after	over	to	around
beneath	along	behind	before	below	on	at	against
beyond	between	across	until	about	out	in	into

Prepositional Phrases

during the concert	across the street	behind the couch
at school	on the field	at the party
after the game	on Tuesday	in her sleeping bag

Whole Group Let's use prepositional phrases in sentences.

A. Use the prepositions or the prepositional phrases from the box to help you complete each sentence. A comma should be used after each prepositional phrase.

1. _____ the children worked hard to create the mural of a city.

2. _____ everyone was planning the celebration.

3. _____ Alexis felt warm and toasty.

4. _____ Dyana sang the silliest song she had ever heard.

5. _____ Andrew could see all his friends playing baseball.

B. Below, only the prepositional phrase is given. Complete each sentence.

1. **Beneath the tall bridge,** _____ .

2. **Along the sidewalk,** _____ .

3. **Behind the school,** _____ .

4. **During the rainstorm,** _____ .

5. **From the window,** _____ .

Begin a Story with a Prepositional Phrase

A writer can use prepositional phrases to include important information at the beginning of a story. A prepositional phrase begins with a preposition and ends with a noun or pronoun. These phrases can answer the questions *where*, *what kind*, *which one*, *when*, and *how*.

Prepositions

above	during	under	by	after	over	to	around
beneath	along	behind	before	below	on	at	against
beyond	between	across	until	about	out	in	into

Whole Group Let's write an opening paragraph that begins with a prepositional phrase.

Brainstorming Time!

A. Complete each of the phrases by beginning it with a preposition from the box. Include any necessary words between the preposition and the noun to finish the phrase.

_____ **bench**   _____ **giraffe**

_____ **tree house**   _____ **playground**

B. Write opening sentences with two of the prepositional phrases from Part A.

1. _____

2. _____

Independently Now put together your opening paragraph.

A. Choose one of the openers from Part B above. Then make a list of events you want to include in the paragraph. The events should be in the order in which they will appear.

1. _____   3. _____

2. _____   4. _____

B. Write an opening paragraph using the sentence you chose and the events from above.

_____

_____

_____

Check Your Work

What question did your prepositional phrase answer?

Whole Group Share your paragraph with the class.

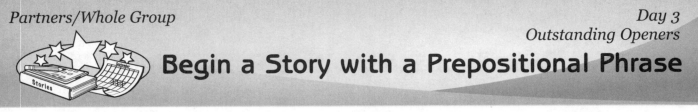

Begin a Story with a Prepositional Phrase

Prepositional phrases answer the questions: *where, what kind, which one, when,* and *how.* Writers often use prepositional phrases to add details in order to expand sentences.

Prepositions

above	during	under	by	after	over	to	around
beneath	along	behind	before	below	on	at	against
beyond	between	across	until	about	out	in	into

Partners Working with a partner, circle all the prepositional phrases in the paragraph.

The Neighborhood Garden

In my neighborhood, there is a beautiful flower garden where everyone has their own special place. Mrs. Cook's garden is beyond the front gate. In her garden, there are tall sunflowers with bright yellow petals. Mr. Walker planted roses against the back fence. The roses climb along the crooked fence, creating a wall of color. During the evening, the children enjoy looking at the flowers and running through the sprinklers.

Whole Group Share the prepositional phrases that you circled.

Partners With a partner, expand the following sentences with prepositional phrases. The prepositional phrase can be at the beginning, middle, or end of each sentence.

Example: *The boys built a clubhouse.*   *The boys built a clubhouse with old lumber.*

1. Samantha completed an art project.

   _____

2. The boys watched a bicycle race.

   _____

3. Oscar ran as fast as he could.

   _____

4. Jonathan opened the box.

   _____

Check Your Work

Where did you place the prepositional phrases in the sentences?

Whole Group Share one expanded sentence with the class.

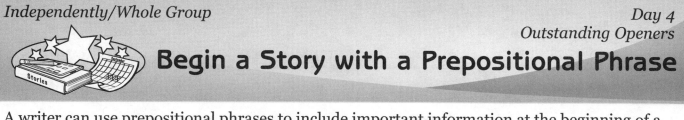

Begin a Story with a Prepositional Phrase

A writer can use prepositional phrases to include important information at the beginning of a story. These phrases can answer the questions: *where, what kind, which one, when,* and *how.* A prepositional phrase begins with a preposition and ends with a noun or pronoun.

Independently Write an opening paragraph using a prepositional phrase.

A. Write opening sentences using two of the following prepositional phrases.

at the door   under the bed

across the ocean   through the tunnel

1. _____

2. _____

B. Select one of the above sentences for an opening paragraph. Which prepositional phrase sentence would make the best opener?

Number _____ would make the best opener because _____.

C. Make a list of events to include in the paragraph. The events should be written in the order they will appear in the paragraph.

1. _____   3. _____

2. _____   4. _____

D. Write an opening paragraph with the prepositional phrase opener you selected and the events from Part C. You can also use prepositional phrases throughout the paragraph.

_____

_____

_____

_____

_____

_____

Check Your Work

What question did the opening sentence answer?

Did you use prepositions anywhere else in the paragraph?

Whole Group Share your paragraph with the class.

Begin a Story with a Prepositional Phrase

A writer can use prepositional phrases to include important information at the beginning of a story. A prepositional phrase begins with a preposition and ends with a noun or pronoun. Prepositional phrases expand sentences by adding details. These prepositional phrases can answer the questions *where, what kind, which one, when,* and *how.*

Independently Write an opening paragraph beginning with a prepositional phrase.

Prepositions

above	during	under	by	after	over	to	around
beneath	along	behind	before	below	on	at	against
beyond	between	across	until	about	out	in	into

Prepositional Phrase Openers

After the game, I couldn't stop thinking about the last play.

For the parade, I was supposed to wear my uniform.

On the papers, Marie found a peculiar message.

A. Choose or create an opening sentence that includes a prepositional phrase. Write it here.

_____

B. Make a list of events to include in the paragraph. The events should be written in the order they will appear in the paragraph.

1. _____   3. _____

2. _____   4. _____

C. Write an opening paragraph with the prepositional phrase opener from part A and the events from Part B. You can use prepositional phrases throughout the paragraph.

_____

_____

_____

_____

Check Your Work

What information did the reader learn from the opening phrase?

Whole Group Share your paragraph with the class.

Add Transitions to Connect Beginning Ideas

Transitions are words and phrases that can be used to connect ideas throughout a story. They can indicate the sequence, a purpose, or a contrast between ideas. Transitions are often used to combine simple sentences to create longer ones. Transitional words or phrases can be used to begin a sentence or paragraph. Transitions can be used anywhere to link one thought to another.

Example

"Oh, boy! Camp starts tomorrow!" exclaimed Andy. Andy was busy packing his clothes and equipment for his month stay at sleep-away camp. He could hardly wait for the next day to come.

As soon as Andy woke up, *he ran out to the car with all of his things. However, the car was locked because his parents were still asleep. He yelled for them to wake up, so they could get ready to go.*

Sequence, Purpose, and Contrast Transitions

first	to start with	as soon as	before	for that reason	just as
so that	otherwise	however	instead	in the same way	but
now	earlier	presently	shortly	in the beginning	currently

Whole Group Use transitional words or phrases from the box to complete each sentence. The transitions must make sense with the rest of the sentence.

1. _____, we should buy the decorations we need for the dance.

2. _____ today, my family visited my grandparents, _____ we do every Sunday.

3. _____, the class will be learning fractions; _____ we can move on to decimals.

Independently Write transitional words or phrases from the box to complete the sentences.

1. _____ , I am practicing for the school play. _____ I cannot come over to your house today.

2. _____ Stanley had his test, he thought he knew everything. _____ he is not sure.

3. _____ Teri sets the table, we will eat.

Whole Group Share one of the sentences with the class.

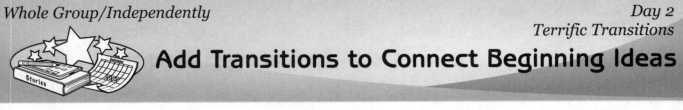

Add Transitions to Connect Beginning Ideas

Connect ideas throughout a story by using transitional words and phrases. Transitional words and phrases can indicate the sequence, a purpose, or a contrast between ideas.

Sequence, Purpose, and Contrast Transitions

first	to start with	as soon as	before	for that reason	just as
so	otherwise	however	instead	in the same way	but
now	earlier	presently	shortly	in the beginning	currently

Whole Group Let's get ready to add a transition and second paragraph to the paragraph below.

"Screech!" The sound from Sandy's flute made everyone cover their ears.
Sandy was so excited when she learned that she was going to play the flute.
She sat in front of the teacher and played her first note. It was awful!

A. Create a list of transitional words or phrases that could begin the next paragraph.

1. _____   3. _____

2. _____   4. _____

B. Write sentences using two of the transitional words or phrases in Part A. Transitional words and phrases can go anywhere in the sentence.

1. _____

2. _____

Independently Now, write the paragraph.

A. Choose one of the sentences to begin the next paragraph. Then, make a list of events to include in the paragraph.

1. _____   3. _____

2. _____   4. _____

B. Using the sentence you chose and the events in Part A, continue Sandy's story.

_____

_____

_____

Check Your Work

Did you use transitional words and phrases throughout the paragraph?

Whole Group Share your paragraph with the class.

Add Transitions to Connect Beginning Ideas

Transitional words and phrases can indicate the sequence, a purpose, or a contrast between ideas. Connect ideas throughout the story by using transitional words and phrases.

> ## Sequence, Purpose, and Contrast Transitions
>
> | | | | | | |
> |---|---|---|---|---|---|
> | first | to start with | as soon as | before | for that reason | just as |
> | so | otherwise | however | instead | in the same way | but |
> | now | earlier | presently | shortly | in the beginning | currently |

Partners With a partner, write sentences that include transitions.

A. Add transitional words or phrases from the box to the sentences below. Then finish each sentence by including an additional thought.

Example: *Dad and I went to the store.*

*Dad and I went to the store **before** we watched the football game.*
(transition)   (additional thought)

Transition   **Additional Thought**

1. Tim studied for the math test _____ .

2. I have to wash the dog _____ .

3. My mom is so unfair, _____ .

B. Combine two complete thoughts using the transitional words or phrases provided below. The thoughts must make sense with the transitions.

1. _____ , **but** _____ .

2. _____ , **so that** _____ .

3. _____ , **before** _____ .

Independently On your own, combine two complete thoughts using the transitional words or phrases provided below. The thoughts must make sense with the transitions.

1. _____ , **or** _____ .

2. _____ , **as soon as** _____ .

Whole Group Share one of the sentences with the class.

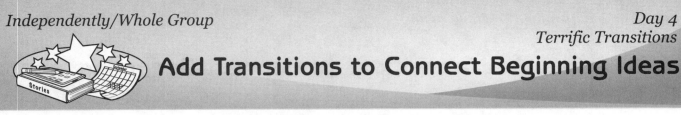

Add Transitions to Connect Beginning Ideas

Transitional words and phrases can indicate the sequence, a purpose, or a contrast between ideas. Connect ideas throughout the story by using transitional words and phrases. Transitional words or phrases can be used to begin a sentence or paragraph. Transitional words and phrases can be used anywhere to link one thought to another.

Sequence, Purpose, and Contrast Transitions

first	to start with	as soon as	before	for that reason	just as
so	otherwise	however	instead	in the same way	but
now	earlier	presently	shortly	in the beginning	currently

Independently Read the opening paragraph. Then, add a transition and second paragraph.

"I thought Kyra was my best friend," cried Kaitlin. "How could she betray me like this?" Kyra always met Kaitlin before lunch, but now Kyra was at a table talking to the new girl, Margie.

A. Using the transitional words and phrases below, complete each sentence for the beginning of the next paragraph.

  1. **To start with,** _____ .

  2. **As soon as** _____ .

  3. **Earlier,** _____ .

B. Select one of the above sentences to begin the second paragraph. Which one would be the best beginning for that paragraph?

  The best sentence for the second paragraph is number _____ because _____ .

C. Make a list of events to include in the paragraph. The events should be written in the order they will appear in the paragraph.

  1. _____   3. _____

  2. _____   4. _____

D. Write the next paragraph with the sentence you selected from Part A and the events from Part C. Make sure this paragraph flows smoothly from the opening paragraph.

Check Your Work

Does the sentence you selected make your story flow from one paragraph to the next?

Whole Group Reread the opening paragraph, then share your paragraph with the class.

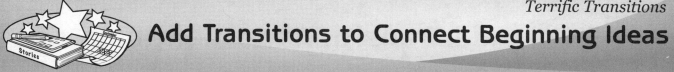

Add Transitions to Connect Beginning Ideas

Connect ideas throughout the story by using transitional words and phrases. Transitional words and phrases can indicate the sequence, a purpose, or a contrast between ideas.

Independently Read the opening paragraph. Then create a second paragraph that includes transitional words or phrases.

The house looked empty. Where was everyone? Jerome's dad said to be home by five o'clock so that he could go to get a haircut. Well, Jerome was here, but where was his dad?

Transitional Sentences

First, Jerome had to beg Eddie's brother to drive him home.

As soon as Jerome saw what time it was, he started to panic.

Before coming home, Jerome had to eat a huge hamburger and a salad in two minutes.

Sequence, Purpose, and Contrast Transitions

first	to start with	as soon as	before	for that reason	just as
so	otherwise	however	instead	in the same way	but
now	earlier	presently	shortly	in the beginning	currently

A. Write a sentence that includes a transitional word or phrase of your choice, or select a sentence from the box. Write the sentence you will use to begin your paragraph.

_____

B. Make a list of events to include in the paragraph. The events should be written in the order that they will appear in the paragraph.

1. _____   3. _____

2. _____   4. _____

C. Write the next paragraph using the sentence from Part A and the events in Part B. Use transitional words and phrases to connect your ideas and make your story flow.

_____

_____

_____

Check Your Work

Are your ideas flowing from one paragraph to the next?

Whole Group Reread the opening paragraph, then share your paragraph with the class.

Add Transitions to Continue Ideas

Writers use transitional words and phrases to join thoughts, sentences, and paragraphs. Transitions connect ideas in a logical and understandable way, so the reader can follow the events of the story to the end. Using transitional words and phrases in a story will improve the connection of ideas.

Example

"Oh, boy! Camp starts tomorrow!" exclaimed Andy. Andy was busy packing his clothes and equipment for his month stay at sleep-away camp. He could hardly wait for the next day to come.

__As soon as Andy woke up,__ he ran out to the car with all of his things. However, the car was locked because his parents were still asleep. He yelled for them to wake up, so they could get ready to go.

__After__ his parents got up, Andy packed everything in the car, ate, and said goodbye to his dog. __Eventually,__ he was in the car and on his way to camp.

Transitional Words and Phrases

first	even so	for example	meanwhile	afterward	soon
second	at last	although	rather than	finally	eventually
still	to start with	however	for instance	besides	also
then	initially	next time	even though	usually	and yet

Whole Group Complete the following sentences with transitional words or phrases from the box.

1. The school bus drove away, _____ I was not on it.

2. _____, Lauren wrote an amazing play about living on Mars.

3. The doctor checked the boy's temperature. _____, she gave him some medicine.

Independently Write a transitional word or phrase from the box to complete the sentences.

1. _____, Kate thinks writing a story is easier than solving math problems.

2. The dog never barks, _____ there are strangers at the door.

3. _____, my baby sister makes a mess when she eats by herself.

Whole Group Share one of the sentences with the class.

Add Transitions to Continue Ideas

Transitional words and phrases join thoughts, sentences, and paragraphs in a logical and understandable way. Transitional words and phrases can be used in the middle of a story to bridge the ideas in the first paragraph to the ideas in the final paragraph.

Transitional Words and Phrases

first	even so	for example	meanwhile	afterward	soon
second	at last	although	rather than	finally	eventually
still	to start with	however	for instance	besides	also
then	initially	next time	even though	tomorrow	and yet

Meow! Meow! I looked up and saw a small, black kitten up in a tree in my back yard. I knew it was in trouble.

__At first,__ I tried to coax it down, but I realized the kitten was not going to come down by itself. It looked scared and helpless; __for that reason,__ I decided to go for help.

Whole Group What do you think will happen to the kitten? Write sentences that could begin the next paragraph using the transitional words and phrases below. The transitional words and phrases can be placed anywhere in the sentence.

1. **usually:** _____

2. **eventually:** _____

3. **even though:** _____

Independently Now continue the story using transitional words and phrases.

A. Choose one of the sentences to begin the next paragraph, and circle it.

B. Make a list of events to include in the paragraph.

   1. _____   3. _____

   2. _____   4. _____

C. Using the sentence you chose and the events in Part B, continue the story on a separate piece of paper.

Check Your Work

Did the transitional words and phrases connect ideas throughout the paragraph?

Whole Group Reread the paragraphs above, then share your new paragraph with the class.

Add Transitions to Continue Ideas

Transitional words and phrases are used to move the story along smoothly. Ideas are connected and flow from one sentence or paragraph to the next. Without transitional words and phrases, a reader would have difficulty following the events in a story.

Transitional Words and Phrases

first	even so	for example	meanwhile	afterward	soon
second	at last	although	rather than	finally	eventually
still	to start with	however	for instance	besides	also
then	initially	next time	even though	tomorrow	and yet

The following paragraphs do not contain transitional words and phrases.

"Yuck! My hair looks awful!" I complained. I had told the barber to take a little off, not make me bald. Why don't people listen to me?

I should have known that it was going to be one of those days. My little sister took my favorite video game. She tried to flush it down the toilet. I screamed at her. My mom yelled at me for yelling at her. Mom did not want to hear my side of the story.

My dog, Dexter, knocked over his dish of food. I had to clean it up. Dexter kept barking at me the entire time I was picking up his food. He tried to bite me. He thought I was stealing it.

Partners Were these paragraphs hard to follow? When you do not use transitional words and phrases, the sequence of the story is difficult to understand. With your partner, rewrite the paragraphs using transitional words and phrases from the list to make the story flow from one event to the next. Use transitional words and phrases to combine sentences and transition from one idea to the next.

_____

_____

_____

_____

_____

Check Your Work

Does the story flow better with the transitional words and phrases that you added?

Whole Group Share your version of the story with the class.

Add Transitions to Continue Ideas

Transitional words and phrases move ideas along in a logical order. They help readers stay on track and will easily follow the events in the story.

Transitional Words and Phrases

first	even so	for example	meanwhile	afterward	soon
second	at last	although	rather than	finally	eventually
still	to start with	however	for instance	besides	also
then	initially	next time	even though	tomorrow	and yet

Independently Read the following paragraphs and add to the story.

What is wrong with him? My brother is always embarrassing me. He goes to school wearing clothes that don't match, two different sneakers, and his hair sprayed purple. I wish people didn't know he is my brother.

In the beginning, I thought it would be great going to the same school as my brother. That was before he started to act strange. Now, I try to hide when I see him.

A. Do you think the situation will get better or worse? Using the transitional words and phrases below, write three sentences that could begin the third paragraph.

　1. **for example:** _____

　2. **although:** _____

　3. **soon:** _____

B. Select one of the above sentences to begin the third paragraph. Which one would be the best beginning for that paragraph?

The best sentence for the third paragraph is number _____ because _____ .

C. Make a list of events to include in the paragraph. The events should be written in the order they will appear in the paragraph.

　1. _____　　　3. _____

　2. _____　　　4. _____

D. On a separate piece of paper, write the third paragraph with the sentence you chose from Part A and the events from Part C. Include other transitional words and phrases.

Check Your Work

Did you include transitional words and phrases in the paragraph?

Whole Group Share your paragraph with the class.

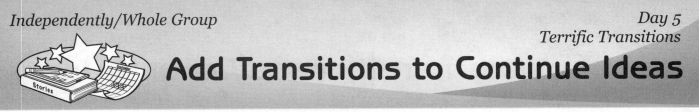

Add Transitions to Continue Ideas

Transitional words and phrases connect ideas to move the story forward in a logical order. Transitional words and phrases are used throughout the story to help the reader understand what is happening.

Independently Read the paragraphs. Then, add to the story.

"You go around the house this way, and I'll go the other way," I screamed. "We will trap him in the middle." Our dog, Dexter, hates getting a bath. Mom told us he needed one because he rolled in the mud and was getting it all over the house.

Before we can give him a bath, *we have to catch him. How does he always know when we are going to give him a bath? We don't even have the tub or the hose out, and yet he is running away from us as fast as he can.*

A. How do you think the children will catch their muddy dog? What do you think they will do? To begin the next paragraph, create a sentence that includes a transitional word or phrase. You can also select a sentence from the box below.

> ### Transitional Sentences
>
> Although I am a fast runner, Dexter is much faster.
>
> Eventually, we caught Dexter by giving him a treat.
>
> Soon, we decided to stop running after him and we came up with a plan.
>
> Usually, it only takes us a few minutes to catch him, even though he is fast.

B. Make a list of events to include in the paragraph. The events should be written in the order they will appear in the paragraph.

1. _____   3. _____

2. _____   4. _____

C. Write the third paragraph about Dexter beginning with the sentence that you chose and the events in Part B. Glue your ideas together by using transitional words and phrases.

_____

_____

_____

_____

> ### Check Your Work
>
> Are the ideas flowing from one paragraph to the next?

Whole Group Share your paragraph with the class.

Add Transitions to End a Story

Writers use transitional words and phrases throughout their stories to connect ideas. Transitional words and phrases help to move ideas and events in a sequential and logical way. Using transitional words and phrases at the end of the story will bring it to a meaningful or exciting conclusion.

In the following paragraphs, transitional words and phrases are connecting ideas so the story flows to the end. Beginning the closing paragraph with the word "finally" helps the reader follow the events to the end.

"Oh, boy! Camp starts soon!" exclaimed Andy. He could hardly wait.

Eventually, *he was in the car and on his way to camp. Andy was thinking about all the fun he would have.*

Finally, *Andy arrived at the camp and leaped out of the car. He spotted his friends from last summer and quickly said good-bye to his parents.* ***At last,*** *his summer adventure was going to begin.*

Ending Transitional Words and Phrases

in conclusion	finally	for this reason	basically	with this in mind
in other words	lastly	most importantly	in closing	as a result
in the end	at last	from that time on	later on	in summary

Whole Group Fill in the blanks using a transitional word or phrase from the box. The transitional words and phrases must make sense with the rest of the sentence.

1. _____ , Nicole decided to run for student council president.

2. The girls' soccer team won a game. _____ , they each got a trophy.

3. _____ , I would like to thank the parents for their support.

Independently Write a transitional word or phrase from the box to make each sentence complete. The transitional word or phrase must make sense with the rest of the sentence.

1. The school cafeteria added a salad bar to the menu; _____ , students can buy a light lunch.

2. _____ , the science fair was a great success.

3. Student behavior improved in the school; _____ , the principal declared Fridays to be "no homework" days.

Whole Group Share one of the sentences with the class.

Add Transitions to End a Story

A writer can use transitional words and phrases to connect ideas throughout a story to the end. Using transitional words and phrases can link earlier events to the ending in a meaningful way.

Ending Transitional Words and Phrases

in conclusion	finally	for this reason	basically	with this in mind
in other words	lastly	most importantly	in closing	as a result
in the end	at last	from that time on	later on	in summary

Whole Group Read the paragraphs. The ideas flow from one paragraph to the next because of transitional words and phrases.

"Excellent!" shrieks Julia. She has just found out that she has been chosen to represent her school in the Regional Spelling Bee.

To start with, Julia creates a plan for preparing for the spelling bee. First, she will study every day after dinner for one hour. Her plan includes asking her teacher for extra help with the spelling rules.

Next, Julia begins her plan. She speaks to her teacher, and of course she agrees to help her. Eventually, she becomes confident that her plan will lead her to success.

Independently Write the final paragraph of the story using transitional words or phrases.

A. Use each of these transitions to write a beginning sentence for the story's final paragraph.

1. **In conclusion,** _____ .

2. **In the end,** _____ .

3. **For these reasons,** _____ .

B. Choose one of the sentences to begin the closing paragraph. Then, make a list of events to include in the paragraph.

1. _____   3. _____

2. _____   4. _____

C. On a separate piece of paper, use the sentence you chose and the events you listed to write the final paragraph about Julia and the spelling bee.

Check Your Work

Did the story come to a logical conclusion?

Whole Group Share your ending paragraph with the class.

Add Transitions to End a Story

Writers use transitional words and phrases to link events in a logical, sequential way. Transitional words and phrases are particularly necessary when writing instructions.

Transitional Words and Phrases

to begin with	first	for example	meanwhile	now
basically	next	most importantly	in closing	however
for instance	after	with this in mind	therefore	especially
consequently	then	finally	otherwise	in addition

Partners Working with a partner, fill in the blanks with transitional words and phrases to complete the how-to essay. Make sure that the essay flows in a logical order.

Steps to Plan a Party

What a great idea! I am giving my best friend a surprise birthday party. Planning a party is fun, but it is a lot of work, too. There are many things to do to get ready. (1) _____ I need to make a list of friends to invite to the party, buy the invitations, and (2) _____ mail them out. (3) _____ I am ready to plan the party. (4) _____ I will decide what to serve at the party, and (5) _____ that I will go shopping. I also need to buy the decorations, (6) _____ the balloons. (7) _____ I will think of a way to get my friend to the party. (8) _____ I need to find the perfect gift. (9) _____ I will be spending some of my time in the mall shopping. I can't wait; this is going to be the best party ever.

Whole Group Share the essay. There is more than one correct answer for most of the blanks.

Partners With your partner, write a how-to essay about the steps you take to clean your bedroom. Include transitional words and phrases so the reader can follow the sequence.

_____

_____

_____

_____

Check Your Work

Do the transitional words and phrases follow a logical order?

Whole Group Share the how-to essay with the class.

Add Transitions to End a Story

Transitional words and phrases move ideas along in a logical way. Transitional words and phrases help readers understand the story by enabling them to connect ideas. Readers can follow the events of the story to the end when transitional words and phrases are used.

Ending Transitional Words and Phrases

in conclusion	finally	for this reason	basically	with this in mind
in other words	lastly	most importantly	in closing	as a result
in the end	at last	from that time on	later on	in summary

Independently Read the following paragraphs. Then create a closing paragraph.

Was that the phone? Matan wanted to hide. His teacher, Mrs. Leon, had told him she would be calling tonight, but he had been hoping she would forget.

Now, his mother was answering the phone. Immediately, the smile left her face. At once, Matan knew that it was Mrs. Leon. Soon, Mom would find out that he hadn't completed his homework all week.

After Mom got off the phone, she marched over to where he was standing. She told Matan that she was disappointed in him and that he was grounded for a week.

A. Using the transitional word and phrase below, complete each sentence for the beginning of the closing paragraph.

   1. **In closing,** _____

   2. **Basically,** _____

B. Select one of the above sentences to begin the last paragraph. Which sentence would be the best one?

   I chose number _____ **because** _____ .

C. Make a list of events to include in the closing paragraph. The events should be written in the order they will appear in the paragraph.

   1. _____   3. _____

   2. _____   4. _____

D. On a separate piece of paper, write the final paragraph about Matan with the sentence from Part A and the events from Part C.

Check Your Work

Did the story come to a logical conclusion?

Whole Group Share your ending paragraph with the class.

Add Transitions to End a Story

A writer can use transitional words and phrases throughout a story. Transitions can be used at the end of the story to bring it to a meaningful or exciting conclusion.

Independently Read the paragraphs. Then, complete the story.

My new shirt is ruined! Mom warned me not to wear it to the ice cream shop, but I wouldn't listen. Chocolate ice cream on a white shirt is the worst.

Originally, I was going to wear my old sweater, but I wanted to show my friends my new shirt. That was a big mistake. Then, I had to tell Mom what happened. Although Mom was angry that I stained my shirt, she still agreed to help me try to get the stain out.

A. Choose or create a sentence that includes a transitional word or phrase of your choice. This sentence will begin the last paragraph. Use the list of transitional words and phrases to help you create your own sentence or select a sentence from the list below.

> ## Transitional Words and Phrases
>
> | | | | |
> |---|---|---|---|
> | in conclusion | finally | as a result | basically |
> | with this in mind | in other words | at last | most importantly |
> | for this reason | in the end | in closing | from that time on |
>
> ## Transitional Sentences
>
> Finally, Mom and I got my shirt to look like new.
>
> At last, my shirt looked great.
>
> From that time on, I knew I should listen to my mom.

My Sentence: _____

B. Make a list of events to include in the closing paragraph. The events should be written in the order they will appear in the paragraph.

1. _____   3. _____

2. _____   4. _____

C. On a separate piece of paper, write the closing paragraph beginning with the sentence you chose in Part A and the events in Part B.

> ## Check Your Work
>
> Did you use transitional words and phrases throughout the final paragraph?

Whole Group Reread the paragraphs above, then share your ending with the class.

Close a Story with a Memory

A writer can end a story with a memory so the reader remembers important events that happened in the story. The events in the story can remind the narrator about another memory that shows how he or she feels, or the events can be what the narrator will never forget.

Example: *Finally, I heard the names of the students who won the essay contest. Unfortunately, my name was not called. I was very disappointed when I heard the announcement. I will never forget how I felt at that moment.*

Memory Words and Phrases

always remember	recall	never forget	reminds me	recollection
brings to mind	memory	remind	recollect	memorable
reminded me of	think of	reminisce	unforgettable	call to mind
remember the time	remember	think back to	looking back	keep in mind

Whole Group Let's give these closing paragraphs an ending that is a memory. Use a word or phrase from the box to give the paragraph a memorable closing.

1. Finally, it was my turn at bat. The team needed one run to win. I was so proud of myself when I hit the ball and saw it sail over the fence. We won, and I felt like a hero.

   _____

2. Basically, Brandon thought his mother baked the best cookies in the world. That is why he entered her in the bake-off contest. After the contest, everyone knew it was true.

   _____

Independently Write a memory closing for each of these paragraphs. You can explain that an event has become an important memory or you can describe a related memory.

1. At last, I got home from a horrible day at school. I tried to open the door, but it was locked. Suddenly, I saw a note that told me to go to the neighbor's house. Great. What else could go wrong? _____

   _____

2. In conclusion, my family and I had a wonderful time at the park. We played games all morning and worked up an appetite. We grilled hamburgers for lunch and had watermelon for dessert. _____

   _____

Whole Group Share a memory closing with the class.

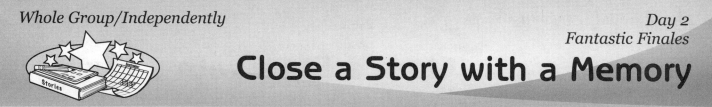

Close a Story with a Memory

A writer can end a story with a memory. The events in the story can become something the character will never forget, or they can remind the character of an important memory.

Memory Words and Phrases

always remember	recall	never forget	reminds me	recollection
brings to mind	memory	remind	recollect	memorable
reminded me of	think of	reminisce	unforgettable	call to mind
remember the time	remember	think back to	looking back	keep in mind

---

Whole Group Let's write a closing with a memory.

A. Below is the first sentence of a closing paragraph. The sentence includes the ending transitional phrase, *with this in mind*, and states the main idea for the paragraph.

With this in mind, Mary had to decide if she really wanted to go to camp.

Write detail sentences that could follow the sentence above.

1. _____

2. _____

B. Write a closing sentence that is a memory. Use the memory words and phrases to help you.

_____

C. On another piece of paper, write the paragraph from beginning to end.

Independently Do you remember a time when you made a new friend? Write a closing paragraph with a memory of this time.

A. Start the paragraph with a main-idea sentence that includes an ending transitional word or phrase, such as *finally*, *at last*, *in conclusion*, or *in the end*.

_____

B. Write a memory closing that would make sense with the details in Part A.

_____

C. On a separate sheet of paper, write the paragraph from beginning to end.

Check Your Work

Do the detail sentences make sense with the memory closing?

Whole Group Share your paragraph with the class.

Close a Story with a Memory

People do not always rely on their memories to keep track of information and experiences. Instead, they write things down so they will not forget them. Keeping a written log is one way to do this. Logs contain the dates, steps, and how long it took you to do a project or a task. You can also include why you did each step and what you learned from the activity.

Example

April 14

My partner and I prepared for the experiment today. We gathered the materials and tools that we needed. My partner and I determined how much of each item we would use. We also decided in what order we would do the steps. It took one hour to prepare for the experiment.

Partners With your partner, read the example, then create a log page. Think of a science experiment that you have done in the past. Remember to include the steps that were taken, how long it took, what you learned, and changes that you would make in future experiments.

April 15

_____

_____

_____

Independently Write two log pages for a project that you have done or that you are doing. Include the steps taken, what you learned, and changes that you would make.

_____
(date)

_____

_____

_____

_____
(date)

_____

_____

_____

Check Your Work

Did you remember to include all of the data for the project?

Whole Group Share one of the log pages with the class.

Close a Story with a Memory

A writer can end a story with a memory so the reader remembers important events from the story or from a character's past.

Independently Write a memory closing. The memory words and phrases can be written anywhere in the sentence. You should change the tense of the verb to fit the rest of the story.

Example: *never forget* ➡ *never forgot*

A. Think about a time in your past when something special happened with your family. Did you go somewhere? Was it a holiday celebration? Did something extraordinary happen? Write closing sentences with the given memory words or phrases on the lines below.

1. **always remember:** _____

2. **reminds me:** _____

3. **looking back:** _____

B. Select one of the above closings to end a paragraph and circle it.

C. Now make a list of events to include in the paragraph. The events should be written in the order they will happen in the paragraph.

1. _____   3. _____

2. _____   4. _____

D. Write an ending paragraph that begins with an ending transitional word or phrase, such as *finally*, *at last*, *in conclusion*, or *in the end*. Use the events from Part C to continue the paragraph. End the paragraph with the memory closing you selected from Part A. The closing should make a lasting impression on the reader.

_____

_____

_____

_____

_____

_____

Check Your Work

Is the closing memorable?

Whole Group Share the closing paragraph with the class.

Close a Story with a Memory

A writer can end a story with a memory. The events in the story can be so meaningful that they become something the character will never forget, or the events can remind the character of an important memory.

Memory Words and Phrases

always remember	recall	never forget	reminds me	recollection
brings to mind	memory	remind	recollect	memorable
reminded me of	think of	reminisce	unforgettable	call to mind
remember the time	remember	think back to	looking back	keep in mind

Memory Endings

My memory of that day . . .   I recall how . . .

This will always remind me of . . .   When I think back to . . .

Independently Write a closing paragraph, ending it with a memory. You can use one of the memory endings to start the final sentence, or you can come up with one of your own.

A. Write the memory closing for your paragraph. This will be the last sentence in the paragraph.

_____

B. Now, make a list of events to include in the paragraph. The events should be written in the order they will happen in the paragraph.

1. _____   3. _____

2. _____   4. _____

C. Write a closing paragraph using the events and memory above. Begin the paragraph with an ending transitional word or phrase, such as *finally*, *at last*, or *in the end*.

_____

_____

_____

_____

Check Your Work

Will the reader understand why the event was special?

Is your closing a memorable one?

Whole Group Share your paragraph with the class.

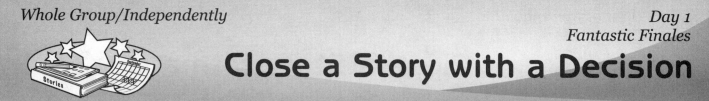

Close a Story with a Decision

People are always making decisions, and so are story characters. A writer can end a story with a decision the character has made based on earlier events in the story. This gives the reader an opportunity to understand the character's thinking and to agree or disagree.

Example: *At last, my mom picked me up from soccer practice. I was in a hurry to get my cleats off, and I didn't put on my seatbelt. All of a sudden, the car swerved, and I fell to the floor. From now on, I will always wear my seatbelt.*

Decision Words and Phrases

because of that	I will never	I will always	as a result
made up my mind	determine	since this time	resolve
therefore, I decided	conclusion	hereafter I will	concluded
after what happened	decided	from now on	choice

Whole Group Write a decision ending for each of the closing paragraphs. The decision must make sense with the rest of the paragraph. Use a word or phrase from the box.

1. **After homeroom, Ed heard that Jake was having a party, and he hadn't received an invitation. He was hurt and upset. Ed started to say mean things about Jake to all his friends. Then he saw Jake coming down the hall. Jake said, "Where have you been? I've been trying to give this invitation to you all day."**

   _____

2. **Michael invited Tim over to play catch, but Tim told him he had too much homework. The truth was that Tim wanted to go bowling with another friend. At the bowling alley, Tim looked up and saw Michael in the next lane.**

   _____

Independently Write a decision closing for each of the paragraphs below. The decision must make sense with the rest of the paragraph. Use the decision words and phrases from the box to help you.

1. **Most importantly, Angie was responsible for taking care of her puppy. She was watching her favorite television show and ignored her puppy's cries. When Angie's show was over, she found a mess on her parents' new carpet.**

   _____

2. **Lastly, my friend came over and was running all around the house acting wild. I didn't tell him to stop. Then he ran into the table, and the vase crashed to the floor.**

   _____

Whole Group Share one of your decision closings with the class.

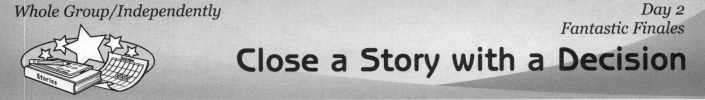

Close a Story with a Decision

People are always making decisions, and so are story characters. A writer can end a story with a decision the character has made based on earlier events in the story. This gives the reader an opportunity to understand the character's thinking and to agree or disagree.

Decision Words and Phrases

because of that	I will never	I will always	as a result
made up my mind	determine	since this time	resolve
therefore, I decided	conclusion	hereafter I will	concluded
after what happened	decided	from now on	choice

Whole Group Below is the first sentence of a closing paragraph. The sentence includes the ending transitional phrase, *in conclusion*, and states the main idea for the paragraph.

In conclusion, Steve decided he was sorry that he had listened to his friend.

A. Write detail sentences that could follow the sentence above.

1. _____

2. _____

3. _____

B. Write two decision closing sentences. Use the decision words and phrases from the list to help you.

1. _____

2. _____

Independently Choose your favorite decision closing. Then, write the paragraph from beginning to end using the sentence given, the detail sentences, and the closing sentence.

_____

_____

_____

_____

Check Your Work

Do the detail sentences make sense with the decision closing?

Whole Group Share the closing paragraph.

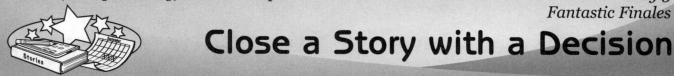

Close a Story with a Decision

People are always making decisions, and so are story characters. A writer can end a story with a decision the character has made based on earlier events in the story. This gives the reader an opportunity to understand the character's thinking and to agree or disagree.

Partners It is not always easy to make a decision. Sometimes people have to make difficult choices. With your partner, read the following situations. Together, write decisions that would solve the problem in each of the situations below.

1. **Betty is trying out for a part in the school play. She just found out her best friend wants the same part. What should Betty do? Why?**

   _____

   _____

2. **Bob sees a classmate take something off his teacher's desk and put it in his pocket. What should Bob do? Why?**

   _____

   _____

3. **Estelle was supposed to bring in the food coloring for the science experiment, but she forgot it. What should Estelle do? Why?**

   _____

   _____

Whole Group Share the decisions that you and your partner made.

Independently Read the following situation and write a decision ending to solve the character's problem.

Mom gave David permission to decorate his room any way that he wanted to. Now she is buying things for the room that he doesn't want. What should David do? Why?

_____

_____

_____

_____

┌ ┄ ┄ ┄ ┄ ┄ ┄ ┄ ┄ ┄ ┄ ┄ ┄ ┄ ┄ ┄ ┄ ┄ ┐

Check Your Work

Did you make good decisions?

└ ┄ ┄ ┄ ┄ ┄ ┄ ┄ ┄ ┄ ┄ ┄ ┄ ┄ ┄ ┄ ┄ ┄ ┘

Whole Group Share your decision ending.

Close a Story with a Decision

People are always making decisions, and so are story characters. A writer can end a story with a decision the character has made based on earlier events in the story. This gives the reader an opportunity to understand the character's thinking and to agree or disagree.

Independently Think about a time when you had to make a decision between doing the right thing and the fun thing. Were you supposed to do a chore and you played instead? Did you go to your friend's house instead of working on a school project? Write a closing paragraph with a decision.

A. Write a closing sentence with the decision words or phrases on the lines below. The decision words and phrases can be written anywhere in the sentence.

1. **from now on:** _____

2. **therefore, I decided:** _____

3. **I will never:** _____

4. **after what happened:** _____

B. Select one of the above closings to be the last sentence in the paragraph. Which decision closing would make the best ending?

The decision closing that will make the best ending is number _____ *because* _____
_____ .

C. Now make a list of events to include in the paragraph. The events should be written in the order they will happen in the paragraph.

1. _____   3. _____

2. _____   4. _____

D. Write a closing paragraph that begins with an ending transitional word or phrase, such as *finally*, *in conclusion*, or *in the end*. Use the events and the decision closing above.

_____

_____

_____

_____

Check Your Work

Does the closing make the reader think about the decision?

Did you begin your closing paragraph with a transitional word or phrase?

Whole Group Share the closing paragraph.

Close a Story with a Decision

People are always making decisions, and so are story characters. A writer can end a story with a decision the character has made based on earlier events in the story. This gives the reader an opportunity to understand the character's thinking and to agree or disagree.

Decision Words and Phrases

because of that	I will never	I will always	as a result
made up my mind	determine	since this time	resolve
therefore, I decided	conclusion	hereafter I will	concluded

Decision Endings

After that day, I was determined to . . .   Before the race, I decided . . .

After what happened, I will always . . .   My choice was . . .

Independently Write a closing paragraph, ending it with a decision. Start the last sentence with any of the decision words or phrases above or use a decision word or phrase of your own. You can also use one of the decision endings above to start the final sentence.

A. Write the ending decision sentence for the paragraph. This will be the last sentence in the paragraph.

_____

B. Now, make a list of events to include in the paragraph. The events should be written in the order they will happen in the paragraph.

1. _____   3. _____

2. _____   4. _____

C. Write a closing paragraph. Begin the paragraph with a sentence that includes an ending transitional word or phrase, such as *finally*, *at last*, *in conclusion*, or *in the end*. Include the events and decision ending from above. The decision ending should give the reader the chance to agree or disagree with the choice.

_____

_____

_____

Check Your Work

Do you think the reader will agree or disagree with the decision?

Did you begin your closing paragraph with a transitional word or phrase?

Whole Group Share the closing paragraph.

Close a Story with a Wish

A writer can end a story with a wish, having a character hope for something wonderful or exciting to happen. Writing a wish at the closing of a story has the reader hoping that the character will experience a happy outcome.

Example: *Tiffany was still dripping wet and out of breath as she watched the swimmers receive their medals. She had trained hard for the competition. Tiffany knew she had done her best. She hoped that next time, she would win.*

Wish Words and Phrases

wish	longing	craving	would like	need
hopeful	want	yearning	wish for	look forward to
crave	yearn for	hope	dream	in my daydreams
my goal	imagine	long for	hankering	with any luck

Whole Group Give these closing paragraphs a hopeful ending by closing with a wish. The wish must make sense with the rest of the paragraph. Use a word or phrase from the box to end the paragraph with a wish.

1. In conclusion, going to California was a fantastic vacation. I learned a great deal about this state and had a wonderful time. I can't wait to visit other states and countries.

   _____

2. At last, the baseball field was done. What a mess it had been! Richard had worked for hours to clean up all the trash. When he was done, he looked around and felt proud. The field looked super, and he couldn't wait to see the surprised faces of his teammates.

   _____

3. Finally, Samantha was ready to open her last gift. She had already received a video game from her grandmother and a bike helmet from her friend. But where was the one thing that she had been wanting and hinting for all year? It had to be in this box.

   _____

Independently Write a closing that ends with a wish.

The results were in, and Osvaldo had won the election. Osvaldo had campaigned hard to be the class president. He had made hundreds of promises to his classmates. Suddenly, Osvaldo realized that his work had just begun.

_____

Whole Group Share your closing.

Close a Story with a Wish

A writer can end a story with a wish, having a character hope for something wonderful or exciting to happen. A wish at the closing of a story has the reader hoping for a dream come true.

Wish Words and Phrases

wish	longing	craving	would like	need
hopeful	want	yearning	wish for	look forward to
crave	yearn for	hope	dream	in my daydreams

Whole Group Below is the first sentence of a closing paragraph. The sentence includes the ending transitional phrase, *at last,* and states the main idea for the paragraph.

At last, the game was over.

A. Write details that could follow the sentence above.

1. _____   3. _____

2. _____   4. _____

B. Write a closing sentence that is a wish. Use the wish words and phrases to help you.

_____

C. On separate paper, write out the paragraph as a class.

Independently Did you ever want something very badly? Was it to go to a special place? Was it something you wanted to buy? Write a closing paragraph about wanting something.

A. Write a beginning sentence with a main idea. Include a transitional word or phrase.

_____

B. Make a list of details to include in the closing paragraph.

1. _____   3. _____

2. _____   4. _____

C. Write a wish closing that would make sense with the details in Part B.

_____

D. On a separate sheet of paper, write the paragraph from beginning to end.

Check Your Work

Do the detail sentences make sense with the wish closing?

Whole Group Share your paragraph.

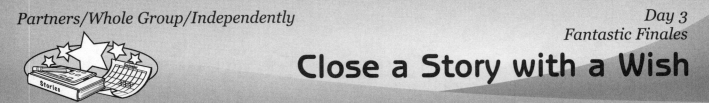

Close a Story with a Wish

A writer can end a story with a wish so the character can hope for something meaningful or special in the future. When you want something, you cannot just wish for it to happen, you must work for what you want. People set goals for obtaining things and work toward them. Someday they hope to achieve their goals.

Partners People of all ages set goals that they want to accomplish. With your partner, think of goals that are appropriate for children your age. Write five goals, and then write a sentence explaining how you would accomplish each one.

Goal 1: _____

_____

Goal 2: _____

_____

Goal 3: _____

_____

Goal 4: _____

_____

Goal 5: _____

_____

Whole Group Share the goals.

Independently People have different goals for themselves. Write a personal goal. What do you want for yourself? Is it something you want to become? Is it something you want to own or a place you want to visit? Write the goal and explain how you will achieve it.

_____

_____

_____

_____

Check Your Work

What will be the most difficult part of achieving your goal?

Why do you think people set goals?

Whole Group Share your goal.

Close a Story with a Wish

A writer can end a story with a wish, having a character hope for something wonderful or exciting to happen. A wish at the closing of a story has the reader hoping for a dream to come true for the character.

Independently Write a closing paragraph, ending it with a wish.

A. Think of something you want to happen. Do you want to be the captain of your team? Do you want to do something special with your family? What will you wish for the next time you blow out your birthday candles? Write a closing sentence with each of the wish words and phrases on the lines below. The wish words and phrases can be written anywhere in the sentence.

1. **hopeful:** _____

2. **with any luck:** _____

3. **look forward to:** _____

4. **want:** _____

5. **hope:** _____

B. Select one of the above closings to end a paragraph. Circle that number.

C. Now make a list of events to include in the paragraph. The events should be written in the order they will happen in the paragraph.

1. _____   3. _____

2. _____   4. _____

D. Write a closing paragraph that begins with an ending transitional word or phrase, such as *finally, at last, in conclusion,* or *in the end.* Use the events and wish closing above.

_____

_____

_____

_____

_____

Check Your Work

Does the closing make the reader think about the character's future?

Did you remember to include a transitional word or phrase in the paragraph?

Whole Group Share the closing paragraph.

Close a Story with a Wish

A writer can end a story with a wish so the character can hope for something wonderful or exciting in the future. Writing a wish at the closing of a story has the reader hoping that the character will experience a happy outcome.

Wish Words and Phrases

wish	longing	craving	would like	need
hopeful	want	yearning	wish for	look forward to
crave	yearn for	hope	dream	in my daydreams
my goal	imagine	long for	hankering	with any luck

Wish Phrases

Next time, I wish I could . . .   Hopefully, I will . . .

I hope I get another chance to . . .   I yearn for the day . . .

Whole Group Write a closing paragraph, ending it with a wish.

A. Write the wish closing for your paragraph. This will be the last sentence.

_____

B. Now make a list of events to include in the paragraph. The events should be written in the order they will happen in the paragraph.

1. _____   3. _____

2. _____   4. _____

C. Write the closing paragraph. Begin the paragraph with a sentence that includes an ending transitional word or phrase, such as *finally*, *at last*, *in conclusion*, or *in the end*. Complete the paragraph by including the events and wish ending above.

_____

_____

_____

_____

_____

_____

Check Your Work

Did you start the paragraph with a transitional word or phrase?

Does the ending have the reader looking forward to happiness for the character?

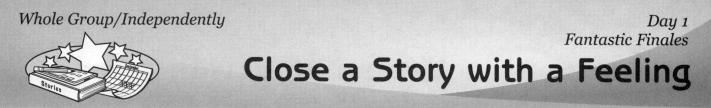

Close a Story with a Feeling

An author can draw the reader into a story by using feelings. A writer can close a story with a feeling so that the reader understands how the story has affected the characters emotionally and infers what action might be taken next.

Example: *Could the last day of school get any better? First, I was thrilled to see I got an "A" on my science test. I had been worried that I would get a bad grade. Then I was excited to find out that I made the soccer team for next year. Finally, my summer vacation was here. I was the happiest person in the world!*

Feeling Words

curious	embarrassed	brave	scared	angry	proud
afraid	furious	happy	sad	shy	guilty
impatient	nervous	delighted	upset	confused	excited

Whole Group End these closing paragraphs by showing how the character is feeling. Use a word from the box to help you end each paragraph with a feeling.

1. Finally, Angie's visit to her grandparents' house was over. She'd had so much fun when her grandmother taught her how to play checkers. She had also enjoyed hearing the funny stories that her grandfather told. She was really going to miss them.

   _____

2. Chrissy had practiced all the routines for weeks and weeks. She knew she had done her best. Now, she was standing behind a group of girls, waiting to hear if she had made the cheerleading team.

   _____

Independently Write a closing sentence that is a feeling for each of the paragraphs below. The feeling must make sense with the rest of the paragraph. Use the feeling words from the box to help you. The closing should have the character expressing an emotion.

1. Samantha's ordeal at the dentist was finally over. Samantha got her new braces on. She decided to get the red ones. As Mom walked into the room, Samantha gave her a big smile.

   _____

2. In the end, Michael knew he had made a big mistake. He should have listened to his friends. He had to admit that this time they were right and he was wrong.

   _____

Whole Group Share one feeling closing.

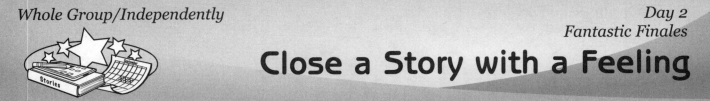

Close a Story with a Feeling

An author can draw the reader into a story by using feelings. A writer can close a story with a feeling so that the reader understands how the story has affected the characters emotionally and infers what action might be taken next.

Feeling Words

curious	embarrassed	brave	scared	angry	proud
afraid	furious	happy	sad	shy	guilty
impatient	nervous	delighted	upset	confused	excited

Whole Group Below is the first sentence of an ending paragraph.

At last, the dark clouds disappeared and the sun was shining.

A. Write details that could follow the sentence above.

1. _____   3. _____

2. _____   4. _____

B. Write a closing sentence that is a feeling. Use the feeling words to help you.

_____

C. On a separate piece of paper, write the paragraph from start to finish as a group.

Independently Do you remember a time when you had to change all your plans because of the weather? Write a closing paragraph about how you felt.

A. Write a main-idea sentence. Include an ending transitional word or phrase in the sentence.

_____

B. Make a list of details to include in the closing paragraph.

1. _____   3. _____

2. _____   4. _____

C. Write a feeling closing that would make sense with the details in Part B.

_____

D. On a separate piece of paper, write the paragraph from beginning to end.

Check Your Work

Do the detail sentences make sense with the closing?

Whole Group Share your paragraph.

Close a Story with a Feeling

Authors write poetry to express feelings in unique ways. A diamante poem is one type of poetry. The seven lines of this kind of poetry form a diamond shape. The purpose of this poem is to describe two subjects that are totally different.

<table>
<tr><td>

Diamante Poem Format

Line 1: One noun that names the 1st subject.

Line 2: Two adjectives describing the 1st subject.

Line 3: Three *-ing* verbs describing the 1st subject.

Line 4: Four nouns, two for each subject, or a short phrase linking the two subjects.

Line 5: Three *-ing* verbs describing the 2nd subject.

Line 6: Two adjectives describing the 2nd subject.

Line 7: One noun that names the 2nd subject.

</td><td>

Example

Bravery

strong, unafraid

helping, protecting, saving

courage, heroism, weakness, anxiety

hiding, crying, escaping

frail, scared

Fear

</td></tr>
</table>

Partners With a partner, write a diamante poem using the feelings *boredom* and *excitement.* Follow the format above. Remember, lines 2 through 6 begin with lowercase letters. A thesaurus would be a valuable resource.

Boredom

_____
(two adjectives)

_____
(three *-ing* verbs)

_____
(four nouns or a phrase)

_____
(three *-ing* verbs)

_____
(two adjectives)

Excitement

Independently On a separate paper, write your own diamante poem about two totally different feelings. Select one of the pairs of feeling words below or think of your own.

Happiness — Sadness   **Pride — Embarrassment**   **Upset — Delight**

Whole Group Share one of the poems.

Close a Story with a Feeling

An author can draw the reader into a story by using feelings. A writer can close a story with a feeling so that the reader understands how the story has affected the characters emotionally. When a story ends this way, the reader can make a personal connection to the feelings of the character.

Independently Think of something important that could spark emotions. Was it a day when everything went right or did everything go wrong? Was it at a special event, such as a field day or a science fair? Was it the best day or the worst day of someone's life?

A. Write a closing sentence with each of the feeling words on the lines below. Feeling words can be written anywhere in the sentence.

1. **excited:** _____

2. **nervous:** _____

3. **lucky:** _____

4. **furious:** _____

5. **embarrassed:** _____

B. Select one of the above closings to end a paragraph. Circle that number.

C. Now make a list of events to include in the paragraph. The events should be written in the order they will happen in the paragraph.

1. _____   3. _____

2. _____   4. _____

D. Write a closing paragraph that begins with an ending transitional word or phrase, such as *finally, at last, in conclusion,* or *in the end.* Use the events from Part C to continue the paragraph. End the paragraph with the feeling closing you selected from Part A. The closing should describe the character's feelings at the end of the story.

_____

_____

_____

_____

Check Your Work

Does the closing express the character's emotions?

Did you begin your closing paragraph with a transitional word or phrase?

Whole Group Share the closing paragraph.

Close a Story with a Feeling

When you express happiness or sadness, you are showing your feelings. A writer can close a story with a feeling so that the reader understands the emotions of the characters at the end of the story.

Feeling Words

curious	embarrassed	brave	scared	angry	proud
afraid	furious	happy	sad	shy	guilty
impatient	nervous	delighted	upset	confused	excited

Feeling Endings

I was delighted to find out . . .   The winning team felt . . .

When the park closed early, Brandon felt . . .   All at once, I felt . . .

Independently Write a closing paragraph, ending it with a feeling.

A. Write the feeling closing for your paragraph. You can use a Feeling Word or Feeling Ending from the box above, or you can come up with one of your own.

_____

B. Now make a list of events to include in the paragraph. The events should be written in the order they will happen in the paragraph.

1. _____   3. _____

2. _____   4. _____

C. Write a closing paragraph. Begin the paragraph with a sentence that includes an ending transitional word or phrase, such as *finally, at last, in conclusion,* or *in the end.* Complete the paragraph by including the events from Part B and the feeling ending in Part A. The closing should express the feelings of the character at the end of the story.

_____

_____

_____

_____

Check Your Work

Does the closing express the character's feelings at the end of the story?

Did you begin your closing paragraph with a transitional word or phrase?

Whole Group Share your paragraph.

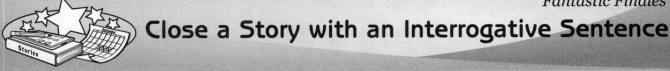

Close a Story with an Interrogative Sentence

An interrogative sentence asks a question. A writer can use interrogative sentences at the end of a story so the reader will question what might happen next or think about important issues the story brings up.

Example: *As a result of what happened at school, I am still thinking about what I did. I wonder if I did the right thing by telling the teacher. I know my friend is not happy with me, but that other boy was really being mean to him. Should I have minded my own business?*

Interrogative Words and Phrases

who	what	where	when	how many	will
how	which	why	whose	which one	am
did	do	is	are	how much	have
were	could	would	was	should	can

Whole Group Use a word or phrase from the box to help you end each paragraph with an interrogative sentence.

1. At last, the recital was over. Noel had practiced the piano every day for weeks. At the recital that night, everything was going great, until he hit the wrong note, again and again.

   _____

2. Finally, the picture was finished. Mary thought it was one of her best paintings. She was so excited when her friend said, "Wow!" when she saw it for the first time.

   _____

3. In other words, Justin's bedroom was a disaster area. He had looked for his cleats for an hour. By the time he found them, he was late for his game.

   _____

Independently Use a word or phrase from the box to help you end the paragraph with an interrogative sentence.

In closing, the first day of school wasn't as bad as I'd thought it would be. My new teacher seems cool and funny. She planned a lot of fun things for us to do. I even like most of the children in my class. I can't believe I actually enjoyed myself.

_____

Whole Group Share the interrogative closing.

Close a Story with an Interrogative Sentence

A writer can use interrogative sentences at the end of a story so the reader will question what might happen next or think about important issues the story brings up.

> ## Interrogative Words and Phrases
>
> | who | what | where | when | how many | will |
> |-----|------|-------|------|----------|------|
> | how | which | why | whose | which one | am |
> | did | do | is | are | how much | have |

Whole Group Below is the first sentence of a closing paragraph. The sentence includes the ending transitional phrase, *for the last minutes*, and states the paragraph's main idea.

For the last minutes of the drive home, Dad let me listen to the music I like.

A. Write details that could follow the sentence above.

1. _____   3. _____

2. _____   4. _____

B. Write a closing interrogative sentence. Use the interrogative words above to help you.

_____

C. On a separate piece of paper, write the paragraph from start to finish as a group.

Independently Think about a time you had to convince your parents to let you do something they didn't want you to do. Write a closing paragraph about how you convinced them.

A. Write a sentence to start the paragraph. Include an ending transitional phrase.

_____

B. Make a list of details to include in the closing paragraph.

1. _____   3. _____

2. _____   4. _____

C. Write an interrogative closing that would make sense with the details in Part B.

_____

D. On a separate piece of paper, write the paragraph from beginning to end.

> ## Check Your Work
>
> Do the detail sentences make sense with the interrogative closing?

Whole Group Share your paragraph.

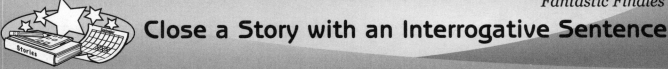

Close a Story with an Interrogative Sentence

An interrogative sentence asks a question. News reporters ask questions when they want to find out information. The questions often begin with *who, what, when, where, why,* and *how.*

Partners BREAKING NEWS! A monkey has escaped from the zoo. News reporters are questioning the zookeeper to find out what happened. With a partner, write interrogative sentences the reporters might ask. Each interrogative sentence will begin with the word given. Write the zookeeper's response below each question.

Example: *(Question) When did the monkey escape?*

(Answer) The monkey escaped before 8 o'clock in the morning.

1. **Who** _____

_____

2. **What** _____

_____

3. **When** _____

_____

4. **Where** _____

_____

5. **Why** _____

_____

_____

6. **How** _____

_____

_____

Independently There's a play in Mrs. Cook's classroom. On a separate piece of paper, write interrogative sentences to get information about the play. Write sentences beginning with *who, what, when, where, why,* and *how.* Then write answers below the questions.

Check Your Work

Did you ask important questions about the play?

Whole Group Share the interrogative sentences and answers for one of the above scenarios.

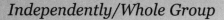
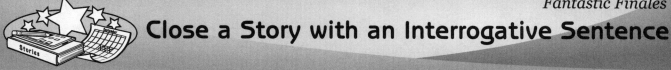

Close a Story with an Interrogative Sentence

Using interrogative sentences at the beginning or the end of a story can spark the reader's interest. A writer can use interrogative sentences at the end of a story so the reader will question what might happen next or think about important issues the story brings up.

Independently Pretend you were invited to a swimming party. Were you anxious or excited? What did you wonder about before you got there? Write an interrogative closing that includes the things you wondered about.

A. Write closing sentences starting with the interrogative words and phrases given below.

1. **Will** _____

2. **How much** _____

3. **Would** _____

4. **When** _____

B. Select one of the above closings to end a paragraph. Which interrogative closing will make the best ending?

The interrogative closing that will make the best ending is number _____ **because** _____
_____ .

C. Now make a list of events to include in the paragraph. The events should be written in the order they will happen in the paragraph.

1. _____   3. _____

2. _____   4. _____

D. Write the closing paragraph. Begin it with an ending transitional word or phrase, such as *finally*, *at last*, *in conclusion*, or *in the end*. Use the events above to continue the paragraph. End the paragraph with the interrogative closing you selected.

_____

_____

_____

_____

_____

Check Your Work

Does the paragraph have the reader wondering about the story's outcome?

Did you begin your closing paragraph with a transitional word or phrase?

Whole Group Share the closing paragraph.

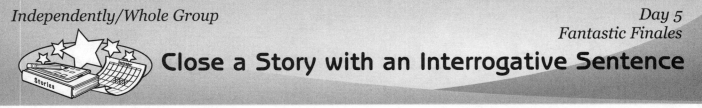

Close a Story with an Interrogative Sentence

Using interrogative sentences at the beginning or the end of a story can spark the reader's interest. A writer can use interrogative sentences at the end of a story so the reader will question what might happen next or think about important issues the story brings up.

Interrogative Words and Phrases

who	what	where	when	how many	will
how	which	why	whose	which one	am
did	do	is	are	how much	have
were	could	would	was	should	can

Interrogative Sentence Starters

Why did I . . .   Am I ever . . .   Should I . . .   Where will he . . .

Independently Write a closing paragraph, ending it with an interrogative sentence.

A. Write the interrogative closing for the paragraph. This will be the last sentence in the paragraph. Use the box above for ideas.

_____

B. Now make a list of events to include in the paragraph. The events should be written in the order they will happen in the paragraph.

1. _____   3. _____

2. _____   4. _____

C. Write the closing paragraph. Begin the paragraph with a sentence that includes an ending transitional word or phrase, such as *finally*, *at last*, *in conclusion*, or *in the end*. Complete the paragraph by including the events and interrogative closing above.

_____

_____

_____

_____

_____

Check Your Work

Did you remember to begin your closing paragraph with a transitional word or phrase?

Whole Group Share your paragraph.

Describe Appearances

Adjectives are words that describe nouns or pronouns. A writer can use physical adjectives to describe the appearance of a character so the reader can envision what the character looks like.

Example: *The black stallion was graceful as it raced across the dusty field. It was galloping away from the tall, strong cowboy who was swinging the lasso.*

Physical Adjectives

plump	awkward	short	tiny	tanned	overweight
chubby	young	old	strong	gawky	small
dainty	athletic	tall	weak	powerful	muscular
huge	slim	sickly	frail	healthy	(hair color)
clumsy	graceful	thin	pale	feeble	(eye color)

Whole Group Add physical adjectives to the following sentences. The words must describe the physical appearance of the characters. Use the physical adjectives in the box to help you.

1. A _____ , _____ ogre was climbing the castle stairs.

2. Mary Ann stared at the _____ , _____ panther.

3. In the middle of the nursery, the _____ , _____ baby was crying.

4. The _____ , _____ dancer tripped on her partner's foot.

5. I saw the _____ , _____ eagle fly over the treetops to its nest.

Independently Practice writing with physical adjectives in the activity below.

A. Think of three nouns and list them on the lines below. Then write two different physical adjectives to describe each noun. Use the box above for help.

1. **Noun:** _____ **Adjectives:** _____

2. **Noun:** _____ **Adjectives:** _____

3. **Noun:** _____ **Adjectives:** _____

B. Write sentences describing each of the nouns above with the physical adjectives.

1. _____

2. _____

3. _____

Whole Group Share your favorite sentence.

Describe Appearances

Adjectives are words that describe nouns or pronouns. A writer can use physical adjectives to describe a character so the reader can envision what the character looks like.

Physical Adjectives

short	tiny	young	strong	gawky	small
dainty	athletic	tall	weak	powerful	muscular
huge	slim	sickly	frail	healthy	(hair color)
clumsy	graceful	thin	pale	tanned	(eye color)

Whole Group Write a paragraph using physical adjectives.

A. Have you ever ridden on a bus? Write physical adjectives that could describe a bus driver. Use the physical adjectives from the box to help you.

1. _____   3. _____

2. _____   4. _____

B. Now write the information requested below about a bus driver. Use physical adjectives from the box or any physical adjectives of your choice.

1. Description of Hair: _____

2. Eye Color: _____

3. Height: _____

4. Description of Clothing: _____

C. Write an Outstanding Opener that will begin a paragraph about the bus driver.

_____

Independently Write a paragraph about a bus driver, using the information above.

_____

_____

_____

_____

Check Your Work

Do the physical adjectives paint a picture of the bus driver?

Whole Group Share your paragraph.

Describe Appearances

Physical adjectives are words that describe the appearance of a character. A writer can use physical adjectives to describe a character so the reader can visualize what the character looks like.

Partners With your partner, use the activities below to practice using physical adjectives.

A. Find and circle the physical adjectives from the box in the word search below. The physical adjectives are written horizontally, vertically, diagonally, backwards, or upside down.

```
A  Z  T  A  N  N  E  D  G  K
D  T  R  Y  Q  J  F  M  N  L
W  I  H  P  M  U  L  P  O  D
G  Q  W  L  N  I  H  T  R  A
E  N  R  W  E  Z  D  M  T  I
S  E  U  F  K  T  G  F  S  N
D  S  H  O  R  T  I  A  T  T
M  G  Z  T  Y  V  E  C  Z  Y
L  U  F  E  C  A  R  G  D  N
L  I  A  R  F  X  L  G  E  D
```

Physical Adjectives

graceful	tanned
young	strong
athletic	dainty
red	frail
short	thin

B. With your partner, write a paragraph about an animal. The animal can be wild or tame; it is your choice. Include as many physical adjectives as you can to describe the animal. Remember to begin the paragraph with an Outstanding Opener.

_____

_____

_____

_____

_____

Independently On a separate sheet of paper, write another paragraph about a different animal. Include physical adjectives that were not already used. Don't forget to begin the paragraph with an Outstanding Opener.

Check Your Work

Do the physical adjectives clearly describe the animal?

Whole Group Share your paragraph.

Describe Appearances

Writers use physical adjectives so the reader can visualize what the character looks like. An author can use adjectives throughout a story to describe any noun.

Physical Adjectives

plump	awkward	short	tiny	tanned	overweight
chubby	young	old	strong	gawky	small
dainty	athletic	tall	weak	powerful	muscular
huge	slim	sickly	frail	healthy	(hair color)
clumsy	graceful	thin	pale	feeble	(eye color)

Independently Write a paragraph using physical adjectives.

A. Look at the nouns below. Write physical adjectives that describe the appearance of each noun. Use physical adjectives from the list or any physical adjectives of your choice.

super hero	baseball player	tiger
1. _____	1. _____	1. _____
2. _____	2. _____	2. _____
3. _____	3. _____	3. _____
4. _____	4. _____	4. _____

B. Select one of the above nouns to use as the main character in a paragraph.

C. Write two Outstanding Openers. Choose one to use as your opening sentence.

1. _____

2. _____

D. Now make a list of events to include in the paragraph. The events should be written in the order they will happen in the paragraph.

1. _____   3. _____

2. _____   4. _____

E. On a separate piece of paper, write a paragraph with the information above. Physical adjectives should also be used to describe any nouns or pronouns in the paragraph.

Check Your Work

Does the paragraph create a clear picture?

Whole Group Share your paragraph.

Describe Appearances

Physical adjectives are words that describe the appearance of a character. The writer creates a vivid and realistic character by using physical adjectives in a story.

Physical Adjectives

short	tiny	young	strong	gawky	small
dainty	athletic	tall	weak	powerful	muscular
huge	slim	sickly	frail	healthy	(hair color)
clumsy	graceful	thin	pale	tanned	(eye color)

List of Characters

a grandparent   a favorite pet   a sports star   a enemy   a alien

Independently Write a paragraph using physical adjectives.

A. Choose a main character from the box, or make one up. List three or more physical adjectives to describe the character.

Character: _____

Physical Adjectives: _____

B. Write an Outstanding Opener for the opening sentence.

_____

C. Now make a list of events to include in the paragraph.

1. _____   3. _____

2. _____   4. _____

D. Write a paragraph with the information above. The physical adjectives should describe the main character and any nouns or pronouns in a paragraph.

_____

_____

_____

_____

Check Your Work

Did you create a vivid and realistic character?

Whole Group Share your paragraph.

Describe Details

Sensory adjectives describe how nouns *look, sound, taste, touch,* and *smell.* A writer can use sensory adjectives to create vivid pictures of the characters, places, and things in a story.

Example: *The bright moon and sparkling stars enabled the hiker to see at night. She quickly walked toward the small, brown cabin and opened the squeaky door. The sweet aroma of cookies baking made her feel safe and warm.*

Sensory Adjectives

Sight:	sparkling	bright	colorful	orange	red	shiny
Sound:	crackling	roaring	whispery	whistling	booming	jangling
Taste:	salty	sweet	spicy	sour	bitter	burnt
Touch:	damp	cool	soft	warm	dull	dry
	rough	sharp	silky	furry	flat	hot
Smell:	fresh	sweet	fishy	perfumed	ripe	musty
	fruity	foul	burnt	spoiled	minty	flowery

Whole Group Add sensory adjectives to the following sentences. The words should create a mental picture for the reader. Use the sensory adjectives in the box to help you.

1. The student gave his teacher a _____ , _____ apple.

2. The _____ , _____ kittens snuggled together.

3. Mom made me take out the _____ , _____ garbage can before I could watch my television show.

Independently Practice writing with sensory adjectives in the activity below.

A. Think of three nouns and list them on the lines below. Write two different sensory adjectives to describe each of these words.

1. **Noun:** _____ **Adjectives:** _____

2. **Noun:** _____ **Adjectives:** _____

3. **Noun:** _____ **Adjectives:** _____

B. Write sentences using the sensory adjectives and the nouns above.

1. _____

2. _____

3. _____

Whole Group Share your favorite sentence.

76

Describe Details

Sensory adjectives include *sight*, *sound*, *taste*, *touch*, and *smell* words. A writer can use sensory adjectives to create vivid pictures of the characters, places, and things in a story.

Sensory Adjectives

Sight:	sparkling	bright	colorful	orange	red	shiny
Sound:	crackling	roaring	whispery	whistling	booming	jangling
Taste:	salty	sweet	spicy	sour	bitter	burnt
Touch:	damp	cool	soft	warm	dull	dry
	rough	sharp	silky	furry	flat	hot
Smell:	fresh	sweet	fishy	perfumed	ripe	musty
	fruity	foul	burnt	spoiled	minty	flowery

Whole Group As a group, prepare to write a paragraph with sensory details.

A. Can you remember the last time you went to the movies? What are some things that you saw, heard, tasted, touched, or smelled? Make a list of things (nouns) that were at the movie theater. Then, write a sensory adjective describing each noun.

1. **Noun:** _____ **Sight Adjective:** _____

2. **Noun:** _____ **Sound Adjective:** _____

3. **Noun:** _____ **Taste Adjective:** _____

4. **Noun:** _____ **Touch Adjective:** _____

5. **Noun:** _____ **Smell Adjective:** _____

B. Now make a list of events to include in a paragraph about going to the movies.

1. _____   3. _____

2. _____   4. _____

C. Write an Outstanding Opener that could begin the paragraph.

_____

Independently On a separate piece of paper, write a paragraph about going to the movies using the information above. Remember to use sensory adjectives throughout the paragraph.

Check Your Work

Do the sensory adjectives help the reader understand the paragraph?

Whole Group Share your paragraph.

Describe Details

Writers can use sensory adjectives to create imagery when they write poems. Imagery in poetry unlocks the meaning of the poem and stimulates the imagination of the reader. The poem below expresses the feeling of anger by using sensory adjectives.

Anger

*Anger is **sizzling**.*
*It is loud and **booming**. (sound)*
*It is **hot** as fire. (touch)*
*It is **foul** and **bitter**. (smell)*
*It is **fiery**. (taste)*
*It is **blazing** like lightning. (sight)*
*Anger is **boiling**.*

Partners With your partner, write a sensory poem about happiness. First, choose a pair of verbs to begin and end the poem from the list below. Write the verbs on lines 1 and 7. Then, use sensory adjectives that describe *sound, touch, smell, taste,* and *sight* to represent happiness. Complete lines 2–6 of the poem using sensory adjectives.

Happiness Verb Pairs

jumping — floating   laughing — cheering   grinning — dancing

Happiness

1. **Happiness is** _____ . (verb)

2. **It is** _____ . (sound)

3. **It is** _____ . (touch)

4. **It is** _____ . (smell)

5. **It is** _____ . (taste)

6. **It is** _____ . (sight)

7. **Happiness is** _____ . (verb)

Independently On a separate piece of paper, write a sensory poem about another emotion. Use words that will create a vivid image in the mind of the reader.

Check Your Work

Do the sensory adjectives create a vivid image?

Whole Group Share one of the poems.

Describe Details

Sensory adjectives can describe *sight*, *sound*, *taste*, *touch*, and *smell*. A writer can use sensory adjectives to create vivid pictures of the characters, places, and things in a story. Sensory adjectives engage the reader and improve reading comprehension.

Sensory Adjectives

Sight:	sparkling	bright	colorful	orange	red	shiny
Sound:	crackling	roaring	whispery	whistling	booming	jangling
Taste:	salty	sweet	spicy	sour	bitter	burnt
Touch:	damp	warm	dry	rough	sharp	silky
Smell:	fresh	sweet	fishy	musty	minty	burnt

Independently Write a paragraph using sensory adjectives to describe details.

A. Write two or three sensory adjectives to describe each of the nouns below. Use sensory adjectives from the list or any sensory adjectives of your choice.

1. **peach:** _____

2. **train:** _____

3. **amusement park:** _____

B. Select one of the nouns from Part A to use as the topic of a paragraph. Circle it.

C. Write an Outstanding Opener to use as the beginning sentence.

_____

D. Now make a list of events to include in the paragraph. The events should be written in the order they will happen in the paragraph.

1. _____   3. _____

2. _____   4. _____

E. Write a paragraph with the information above. The sensory adjectives should create a mental picture of the characters, places, and things throughout the story.

_____

_____

_____

Check Your Work

Do the sensory adjectives help the reader understand the paragraph?

Whole Group Share your paragraph.

Describe Details

Sensory adjectives can describe *sight*, *sound*, *taste*, *touch*, and *smell*. A writer can use sensory adjectives to create vivid pictures of the characters, places, and things in a story. Sensory adjectives engage the reader and improve reading comprehension.

Sensory Adjectives

Sight:	sparkling	bright	colorful	orange	red	shiny
Sound:	crackling	roaring	whispery	whistling	booming	jangling
Taste:	salty	sweet	spicy	sour	bitter	burnt
Touch:	damp	warm	dry	rough	sharp	silky
Smell:	fresh	sweet	fishy	musty	minty	burnt

Story Ideas

playing tennis   a bicycle ride   baking brownies   a holiday   losing a movie ticket

Independently Write a paragraph using sensory adjectives. You may write about any of the story ideas above or think of your own.

A. Choose a topic for your paragraph. Think of things that you could hear, see, taste, touch, and smell. Now, answer the questions below that make sense with your topic.

1. **What could you hear?**_____

2. **What could you see?**_____

3. **What could you taste?** _____

4. **What could you touch?** _____

5. **What could you smell?** _____

B. Write an Outstanding Opener that can begin the paragraph.

_____

C. Now make a list of events to include in the paragraph.

1. _____   3. _____

2. _____   4. _____

D. On a separate piece of paper, write a paragraph with the information above. Include sensory adjectives to describe the characters, places, and things in the paragraph.

Check Your Work

Do the sensory adjectives help the reader understand the paragraph?

Whole Group Share your paragraph.

Describe Feelings

Excited, jealous, and *cheerful* are emotion adjectives. Emotion adjectives are words that express the feelings of characters in a story.

Example: *The grumpy, old woman yelled at the surprised boy as he mistakenly ran across her front yard. The anxious boy was concerned about his lost puppy. He was searching everywhere but could not find his beloved pet.*

Emotion Adjectives

miserable	pleasant	grumpy	excited	sympathetic	doubtful
ecstatic	angry	surprised	anxious	concerned	guilty
jealous	sad	bored	frustrated	confident	suspicious
irritated	cheerful	joyful	frightened	enthusiastic	heartbroken
annoyed	lonely	weary	worried	discouraged	sensitive

Whole Group Add emotion adjectives to the following sentences. The adjectives must describe the feelings of the characters. Use the emotion adjectives in the box to help you.

1. Thomas was _____ when his _____ sister said she didn't have his new game.

2. The _____ police officer tried to help the _____ child find her dad.

3. Today, my _____ , _____ brother kept jumping off the swings.

4. I felt _____ and _____ about joining the Scouts.

5. The _____ dog hid after it ate the _____ girl's dinner.

Independently Practice using emotion adjectives in the activities below.

A. List three characters. Write two different emotion adjectives to describe each one.

1. **Character:** _____ **Adjectives:** _____

2. **Character:** _____ **Adjectives:** _____

3. **Character:** _____ **Adjectives:** _____

B. Write sentences describing the feelings of each character using the adjectives above.

1. _____

2. _____

3. _____

Whole Group Share your favorite sentence.

Describe Feelings

Emotion adjectives are words that express the feelings of characters in a story. Writers use emotion adjectives to make characters more believable so the reader can relate to them.

Emotion Adjectives

miserable	pleasant	grumpy	excited	sympathetic	doubtful
ecstatic	angry	surprised	anxious	concerned	guilty
jealous	sad	bored	frustrated	confident	suspicious
irritated	cheerful	joyful	frightened	enthusiastic	heartbroken
annoyed	lonely	weary	worried	discouraged	sensitive

Whole Group As a group, prepare to write a paragraph using adjectives to describe feelings.

A. Have you ever sat in class next to someone who never stops talking? Write emotion adjectives to describe how you would feel next to a very talkative person.

1. _____   3. _____

2. _____   4. _____

B. Now make a list of events to include in the paragraph about sitting next to a talkative person. The events should be written in the order they will happen in the paragraph.

1. _____   3. _____

2. _____   4. _____

C. Write Outstanding Openers that could begin the paragraph.

1. _____

2. _____

Independently Write a paragraph using the emotion adjectives from Part A. Describe how you would feel if you sat in class next to a person who never stops talking. Begin with an Outstanding Opener from Part C and use the events in Part B to complete the paragraph.

_____

_____

_____

Check Your Work

Can you relate to the character's feelings?

Whole Group Share your paragraph.

Describe Feelings

Some adjectives express emotions. The feelings and thoughts of characters are brought to life when emotion adjectives are used in a story.

Partners An antonym is a word opposite in meaning to another word. Working with a partner, find the antonym for each clue and use it to complete the crossword puzzle. Not all of the words from the Word Box will be used.

Emotion Crossword Puzzle

Word Box

pleasant	miserable
concerned	weary
lonely	doubtful
confident	ecstatic
sensitive	guilty
frustrated	excited
jealous	suspicious

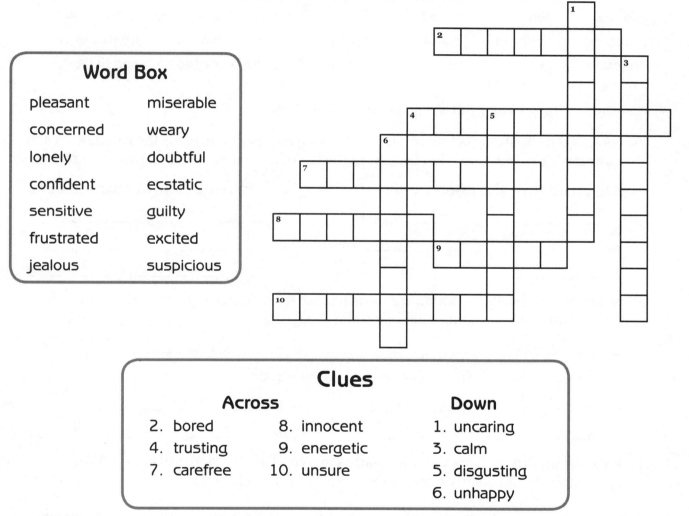

Clues

Across

2. bored
4. trusting
7. carefree
8. innocent
9. energetic
10. unsure

Down

1. uncaring
3. calm
5. disgusting
6. unhappy

Independently Can you remember a time you were in a thunderstorm? Was the thunder loud and scary? Was the lightning exciting? On a separate piece of paper, write a paragraph about being in a thunderstorm. Include emotion adjectives to express how the character is feeling. Remember to begin the paragraph with an Outstanding Opener.

Check Your Work

Do the emotion adjectives clearly express the character's feelings?

Whole Group Share your paragraph.

Describe Feelings

Emotion adjectives are words that express the feelings of characters in a story. Emotion adjectives describe feelings that the reader can relate to.

Emotion Adjectives

miserable	pleasant	grumpy	excited	sympathetic	doubtful
ecstatic	angry	surprised	anxious	concerned	guilty
jealous	sad	bored	frustrated	confident	suspicious
irritated	cheerful	joyful	frightened	enthusiastic	heartbroken
annoyed	lonely	weary	worried	discouraged	sensitive

Independently Write a paragraph using emotion adjectives.

A. Look at the situations below. Write emotion adjectives that express the feelings of each character. Use emotion adjectives from the list or any emotion adjectives of your choice.

Angelina won the poetry contest.

1. _____

2. _____

3. _____

George didn't study for his test.

1. _____

2. _____

3. _____

B. Select one of the above situations to use as the topic of a paragraph. Then, write an Outstanding Opener that could begin the paragraph.

_____

C. Now make a list of events to include in the paragraph.

1. _____

2. _____

3. _____

4. _____

D. Write a paragraph using the information above. The emotion adjectives in the paragraph should clearly express the feelings of the character.

_____

_____

_____

Check Your Work

Does the paragraph clearly express the feelings of the main character?

Whole Group Share your paragraph.

Describe Feelings

Writers can use emotion adjectives to make characters more believable. Emotion adjectives describe feelings that the reader can relate to.

Emotion Adjectives

miserable	pleasant	grumpy	excited	sympathetic	doubtful
ecstatic	angry	surprised	anxious	concerned	guilty
jealous	sad	bored	frustrated	confident	suspicious
irritated	cheerful	joyful	frightened	enthusiastic	heartbroken

Situations

Matthew misses the school bus.   The hockey player loses the game.

You make a gift for your mother.   Krystal moves to a new house.

Independently Write a paragraph using emotion adjectives.

A. Choose a situation from the box or create one of your own. Below, list the main character and three or more emotion adjectives to express how the character feels.

Character: _____

Emotion Adjectives: _____

B. Write an Outstanding Opener that can begin the paragraph.

_____

C. Now make a list of events to include in the paragraph.

    1. _____   3. _____

    2. _____   4. _____

D. Write a paragraph using the information above. The emotion adjectives should express the feelings of the main character or any character in the paragraph.

_____

_____

_____

_____

Check Your Work

Did you express the emotions of the character?

Whole Group Share your paragraph.

Describe Characters

Character traits define a character's personality, behavior, and thoughts. Personality adjectives are words that describe character traits. A writer can use personality adjectives to explain the personality and behavior of a character.

Example: *The gifted student created a new computer game for the class to use. His wise teacher helped her creative student become successful.*

Personality Adjectives

caring	intelligent	gifted	stubborn	thoughtful	loyal
selfish	generous	clever	motivated	affectionate	determined
grumpy	respectful	lazy	impatient	forgiving	courageous
honest	wise	rude	talented	impolite	optimistic
cruel	ambitious	creative	humorous	conceited	adventurous

Whole Group Practice using personality adjectives as a group.

A. Add personality adjectives to the following sentences. Use the box above for help.

1. Ryan was _____ as he waited for his _____ classmate to arrive.

2. The _____ and _____ students participated in the science fair.

3. Sophia was _____ to complete the assignment before her vacation.

4. The _____ artist sold his painting to a _____ customer.

B. Write three personality adjectives to describe the personality of each character below.

Molly the waitress: _____

Jerome the detective: _____

Truong the actor: _____

C. Choose one of the personality adjectives that describes Molly the waitress's personality. Write a sentence using the personality adjective to describe the waitress.

_____

Independently Write sentences with the remaining characters from Part B. Pick one personality adjective to describe each character.

Jerome: _____

Truong: _____

Whole Group Share your favorite sentence.

Describe Characters

Personality adjectives are words that describe character traits. A writer can use personality adjectives to explain the personality and behavior of a character.

Personality Adjectives

caring	intelligent	gifted	stubborn	thoughtful	loyal
selfish	generous	clever	motivated	affectionate	determined
grumpy	respectful	lazy	impatient	forgiving	courageous
honest	wise	rude	talented	impolite	optimistic
cruel	ambitious	creative	humorous	conceited	adventurous

Whole Group As a group, prepare to write a paragraph using personality adjectives.

A. What personality adjectives could describe a good friend? Write adjectives to show the character traits of a good friend. Use the personality adjectives from the box for help.

1. _____   3. _____

2. _____   4. _____

B. Now make a list of events to include in a paragraph about the character traits of a good friend. The events should be written in the order they will happen in the paragraph.

1. _____   3. _____

2. _____   4. _____

C. Write an Outstanding Opener that could begin the paragraph.

_____

Independently Write a paragraph about a good friend. Why is that person a good friend? Use the personality adjectives, Outstanding Opener, and events you listed above.

_____

_____

_____

_____

Check Your Work

Do the adjectives describe the character's personality traits clearly?

Whole Group Share your paragraph.

Describe Characters

Personality adjectives describe a character's personality. A writer can help the reader understand a character's personality by showing the character's negative and positive traits.

Partners With a partner, do the activities below to practice using personality traits.

A. With a partner, read the clues. Then unscramble the letters to find each answer.

Definition	Scrambled Word	Answer
1. determined to succeed	saumobiit	_____
2. unkind to others	elcur	_____
3. artistic	activere	_____
4. refusing to change	butsronb	_____
5. cannot wait	tentimipa	_____
6. overly proud of one's self	dceotniec	_____
7. hopeful	topmistiic	_____
8. courteous to others	flpectseru	_____

B. Look at the answers in Part A. Which personality adjectives describe positive character traits? Circle the positive character traits.

C. With your partner, write a paragraph about a scientist who just invented something. Include the positive personality adjectives you circled in Part A. Remember to begin the paragraph with an Outstanding Opener.

_____

_____

_____

_____

Independently On a separate piece of paper, write a paragraph about a child who tricked a friend. The words from Part A that are not circled are negative personality adjectives. Use these words to write your paragraph. You may also include any personality adjectives of your choice. The personality adjectives should help the reader understand the child's personality. Don't forget to begin the paragraph with an Outstanding Opener.

Check Your Work

Did the adjectives describe the child's personality correctly?

Whole Group Share one of the paragraphs.

Describe Characters

Personality adjectives describe a character's personality. A writer can use personality adjectives to help the reader understand the personality and behavior of a character.

Personality Adjectives

caring	intelligent	gifted	stubborn	thoughtful	loyal
selfish	generous	clever	motivated	affectionate	determined
grumpy	respectful	lazy	impatient	forgiving	courageous
honest	wise	rude	talented	impolite	optimistic

Independently Write a paragraph using personality traits to describe characters.

A. Write personality adjectives that describe each of the characters. Use the box for help.

librarian

1. _____
2. _____
3. _____

dancer

1. _____
2. _____
3. _____

fireman

1. _____
2. _____
3. _____

B. Select one of the above characters to use as the main character in a paragraph.

C. Write an Outstanding Opener that could begin the paragraph.

_____

D. Now make a list of events to include in the paragraph.

1. _____   3. _____
2. _____   4. _____

E. Write a paragraph with the information above. The paragraph should include adjectives that describe the character's personality.

_____

_____

_____

_____

Check Your Work

Does the paragraph describe the character's personality?

Whole Group Share your paragraph.

Describe Characters

Personality adjectives describe character traits. A writer can help the reader understand a character's personality by showing the negative and positive traits of the character.

Personality Adjectives

caring	intelligent	gifted	stubborn	thoughtful	loyal
selfish	generous	clever	motivated	affectionate	determined
grumpy	respectful	lazy	impatient	forgiving	courageous
honest	wise	rude	talented	impolite	optimistic
cruel	ambitious	creative	humorous	conceited	adventurous

List of Characters

a favorite uncle   a neighbor   a cartoon character   a soldier   a coach

Independently Write a paragraph using positive and negative personality adjectives.

A. Choose one of the characters above or create one of your own. Below, list the main character and three or more adjectives to describe the character's personality.

Character: _____

Personality Adjectives: _____

B. Write an Outstanding Opener that could begin the paragraph.

_____

C. Now make a list of events to include in the paragraph.

1. _____   3. _____

2. _____   4. _____

D. Write a paragraph with the information above. The adjectives should show the negative and positive traits of the character.

_____

_____

_____

_____

Check Your Work

Does the paragraph include both positive and negative character traits?

Whole Group Share your paragraph.

Add Similes and Metaphors to a Story

Similes and metaphors are types of figurative language that make comparisons between two things. A simile includes the words "as" or "like" and a metaphor does not. Writers can use similes and metaphors to express things in a more vivid and entertaining way.

Simile Example

*Diana **was as quiet as a mouse** when she heard her brother talking on the telephone. She quickly crept up and hid behind the door to eavesdrop on her brother's conversation.*

Metaphor Example

*Diana **was a mouse** when she heard her brother talking on the telephone. She quickly crept up and hid behind the door to eavesdrop on her brother's conversation.*

Similes	Meanings	Metaphors	Meanings
soft as a pillow	very soft	(was) a train wreck	terrible
hard as a rock	solid and firm	(was) a dolphin	a great swimmer
fresh as a daisy	well rested	(is) a rubber band	very flexible
cool as a cucumber	calm	(is) a brain	very smart

Whole Group Complete the following sentences with similes and metaphors from the box. Circle the two things that are being compared in each sentence.

1. Devin was _____ when he was doing his gymnastic routine.

2. Our team had to stay _____ in order to win the basketball championship.

3. The lifeguard was _____ when he swam out to save the girl.

Independently Rewrite the sentences below and include a simile or a metaphor that would have the same meaning. Remember to use "as" or "like" when you write a simile.

1. Debbie was well rested after her nap.

Simile: _____

_____

2. David's geography project was terrible.

Metaphor: _____

_____

Whole Group Share your sentences.

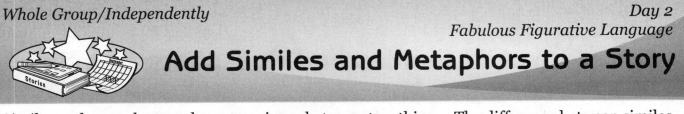

Add Similes and Metaphors to a Story

Similes and metaphors make comparisons between two things. The difference between similes and metaphors is that a simile includes the word "as" or "like" and a metaphor does not. Writers can use similes and metaphors to express things in a more vivid and entertaining way.

Similes	Meanings	Metaphors	Meanings
is as old as the hills	ancient	is a queen bee	act like you are in charge
chatters like a monkey	talks a lot	has clear skies	has no problems
is like a star	bright/talented	spills the beans	tells a secret
eats like a bird	eats a little food	is a rainbow	very colorful
is as slow as a turtle	extremely slow	is a machine	works all the time

Whole Group Write a paragraph using similes and metaphors. The paragraph will be about cleaning a closet. Why did you have to clean the closet? Did you find anything that you had thought was lost forever?

A. Write similes and metaphors that could be used in the paragraph.

Similes

1. _____

2. _____

Metaphors

1. _____

2. _____

B. Think of an Outstanding Opener for the paragraph.

_____

C. Make a list of events to include in the paragraph.

1. _____

2. _____

3. _____

4. _____

Independently Now write the paragraph about cleaning a closet, using the Outstanding Opener and events above. Include one simile and one metaphor from Part A.

_____

_____

_____

_____

Check Your Work

Did the similes and metaphors make the paragraph fun to read?

Whole Group Share your paragraph.

Add Similes and Metaphors to a Story

Similes and metaphors are types of figurative language that compare two different things. These things are not alike in most ways, but have some common connections with each other. A simile includes the words "as" or "like" and a metaphor does not.

Partners Practice identifying and creating similes and metaphors.

A. With a partner, find and underline the simile or metaphor in each of the sentences. Circle the word **simile** if it is a simile or **metaphor** if it is a metaphor. Then, write the meaning of the simile or metaphor on the line.

1. **Molly heard the news and roared like a lion.**

   Simile or Metaphor   Meaning: _____

2. **Carl is like a snail when he does his homework.**

   Simile or Metaphor   Meaning: _____

3. **My computer is a dinosaur.**

   Simile or Metaphor   Meaning: _____

4. **His stomach is a bottomless pit.**

   Simile or Metaphor   Meaning: _____

B. Next, complete the sentences with similes. Then, write the meanings of the similes.

	Simile	**Meaning**
1. The baby was as wiggly as a	_____ .	_____
2. My cat's tongue was as rough as	_____ .	_____
3. He sings like a	_____ .	_____

C. Complete each sentence with a metaphor. Then, write the meaning of the metaphor.

Example: *When I sleep, <u>I am a rock.</u>   <u>I sleep soundly and don't move.</u>*

	Metaphor	**Meaning**
1. When I dance,	_____ .	_____
2. My house is	_____ .	_____
3. When I leap,	_____ .	_____

Check Your Work

Do the similes and metaphors express the thoughts in a vivid way?

Whole Group Share a simile and a metaphor. Tell the meaning of each one.

Add Similes and Metaphors to a Story

Similes and metaphors make comparisons between two things. Writers can use similes and metaphors to express things in a more vivid and entertaining way.

Similes		**Metaphors**	
as soft as a pillow	chatter like a monkey	was a train wreck	is a queen bee
as hard as a rock	as old as the hills	is a dolphin	is a brain
as fresh as a daisy	as slow as a turtle	is bubbly	is a machine
as cool as a cucumber	like a star	is a rubber band	is a rainbow

Independently Write a paragraph with similes and metaphors.

A. Have you ever looked under your bed and discovered something you didn't know was there? What was it? How did it get there? Write down what you found.

I found _____ .

B. Write two similes and two metaphors that could be included in a paragraph about what you found under the bed.

Similes	**Metaphors**
1. _____	1. _____
2. _____	2. _____

C. Think of an Outstanding Opener for the paragraph.

_____

D. Now make a list of events to include in the paragraph.

1. _____	3. _____
2. _____	4. _____

E. Write a paragraph with the information above. Include only the similes and metaphors from Part B that best express your ideas in a vivid and entertaining way.

_____

_____

_____

Check Your Work

Do the similes and metaphors express your ideas in a fun way?

Whole Group Share your paragraph.

Add Similes and Metaphors to a Story

Similes and metaphors make comparisons between things. Writers can use similes and metaphors to express things in a more vivid way.

Similes		Metaphors	
as soft as a pillow	chatter like a monkey	was a train wreck	is a queen bee
as hard as a rock	as old as the hills	is a dolphin	is a brain
as fresh as a daisy	as slow as a turtle	is bubbly	is a machine
as cool as a cucumber	like a star	is a rubber band	is a rainbow

Story Ideas

Helping someone   Skateboarding   Learning the drums   Running for class president

Independently Write a paragraph using similes and metaphors.

A. Choose a story idea above or create one of your own. Write two similes and two metaphors that could be included in the story.

Similes
1. _____
2. _____

Metaphors
1. _____
2. _____

B. Write an Outstanding Opener.

_____

C. Now make a list of events to include in the paragraph.

1. _____
2. _____
3. _____
4. _____

D. Write a paragraph with the information above. Only use the similes and metaphors from Part A that describe things in your paragraph in a vivid way.

_____
_____
_____
_____

Check Your Work

Will the paragraph entertain the reader?

Whole Group Share your paragraph.

Add Idioms to a Story

Lend me your ears; it is time to listen and learn about idioms. *Lend me your ears* is an idiom that means someone wants your attention. An idiom is an expression that means something different from the literal meaning of the phrase. An idiom is a form of figurative language.

Example: *Jonathan was given two weeks to write this report, but he waited until the last day to start it. Now, Jonathan is down to the wire to get it done.*

The idiom *down to the wire* means that someone is running out of time. Using the idiom *down to the wire* makes the writing clever and fun to read.

Idioms	Meanings
under the weather	feeling ill or sick
run out of steam	to be completely out of energy
back to square one	starting over again
he lost his head	he was overcome with anger
make no bones about it	to state a fact so there is no doubt
cry over spilt milk	to complain about the past
a leopard can't change its spots	you cannot change who you are
it cost an arm and a leg	something was very expensive

Whole Group Complete the following sentences with idioms from the box. Both the idiom and its meaning must make sense in each of the sentences.

1. Roni's sister lost her project, and now she is _____ .

2. Jill was _____ when she came home with a sore throat and a headache.

3. My friend wanted to buy a new jacket, but _____ .

4. I worked all day building the doghouse, until I had _____ and had to rest.

Independently Match the idiom with its meaning. Write the correct letter before each idiom.

1. _____ let the cat out of the bag   a. saved at the last moment

2. _____ saved by the bell   b. rushed and short on time

3. _____ a dime a dozen   c. share a secret that shouldn't be shared

4. _____ on the fence   d. common and easy to get

5. _____ against the clock   e. undecided

Whole Group Share your answers.

Add Idioms to a Story

An idiom is an expression that means something different from the literal meaning of the phrase. An idiom is a form of figurative language. Idioms bring interest and fun to a story.

Idioms	Meanings
a drop in the bucket	a small part of something big
add fuel to the fire	to make a bad situation worse
actions speak louder than words	do something instead of just talking about it
all in the same boat	everyone is facing the same challenges
get up on the wrong side of the bed	having a bad day
at the drop of a hat	willing to do something immediately
drive someone up the wall	to irritate or annoy very much
bite your tongue	to avoid talking
get over it	move beyond something that is bothering you

Whole Group Write a paragraph using idioms. It will be about having an argument. Was the argument with a friend or a parent? What could the argument be about?

A. Write idioms that could be used in the paragraph. Use the idioms from the list to help you or any other idioms that you know.

1. _____   3. _____

2. _____   4. _____

B. Write an Outstanding Opener.

_____

C. Make a list of events to include in the paragraph. The events should be written in the order they will appear in the story.

1. _____   3. _____

2. _____   4. _____

Independently On a separate piece of paper, write the paragraph about having an argument. Use the Outstanding Opener, the events, and two of the idioms you listed.

Check Your Work

Do the idioms make the paragraph clever and fun to read?

Whole Group Share your paragraph.

Add Idioms to a Story

An idiom is a form of figurative language. It is an expression that means something different from the literal meaning of the phrase. For example, the idiom *apple of my eye* does not mean there is an apple in your eye. This idiom actually means that someone is cherished above all others. Using idioms brings fun to a story.

Partners Working with a partner, write what you think each idiom means.

Idioms	**Meanings**
1. bend over backwards:	_____
2. from rags to riches:	_____
3. icing on the cake:	_____

Whole Group Share the answers. Correct your mistakes.

Partners Choose one of the idioms above. With your partner, write a paragraph about winning something. Did you win a game or a contest? Draw a line under the idiom.

_____

_____

_____

_____

Whole Group Read the paragraph to the class, omitting the idiom you underlined. Then have the class guess which idiom you used in the paragraph. Were there other idioms that would make sense with the paragraph?

Independently Now write a paragraph about losing something. Did you lose a friend or some money? Use one of the idioms from this page or any idiom that you know.

_____

_____

_____

_____

Whole Group Read your paragraph, omitting the idiom that you underlined. Have the class guess the missing idiom. Could more than one idiom make sense in the paragraph?

Check Your Work

Did your classmates guess the missing idiom?

Add Idioms to a Story

An idiom is an expression that means something different from the literal meaning of the phrase. An idiom is a form of figurative language. Writers can use idioms to express thoughts in clever ways. Idioms bring interest and fun to a story.

Idioms

under the weather	add fuel to the fire	bite your tongue
he lost his head	an arm and a leg	actions speak louder than words
run out of steam	a drop in the bucket	make no bones about it
cry over spilt milk	all in the same boat	drive someone up the wall
back to square one	at the drop of a hat	get up on the wrong side of the bed

Independently Write a paragraph about going on a new amusement park ride.

A. Read the idioms from the list and circle three that you could include in the paragraph. Write a sentence with each of the idioms.

1. _____

2. _____

3. _____

B. Choose one of the sentences from Part A to include in the paragraph. Then, write an Outstanding Opener.

_____

C. Now make a list of events to include in the paragraph.

1. _____   3. _____

2. _____   4. _____

D. Write a paragraph about going on a new amusement park ride with the information above. You can include additional idioms from the list or any idioms of your choice. The idioms you use must make sense in the paragraph.

_____

_____

_____

Check Your Work

Did the idioms express your ideas in a fun way?

Whole Group Share your paragraph.

Add Idioms to a Story

An idiom is an expression that means something different from the literal meaning of the phrase. An idiom is a form of figurative language. Idioms bring interest and fun to a story.

Idioms

under the weather	add fuel to the fire	bite your tongue
he lost his head	an arm and a leg	actions speak louder than words
run out of steam	a drop in the bucket	make no bones about it
cry over spilt milk	all in the same boat	drive someone up the wall
back to square one	at the drop of a hat	get up on the wrong side of the bed

Story Ideas

playing tug-of-war	going to the mall	arguing with a friend	joining a club

Independently Write a paragraph using idioms. Use a story idea above or create your own.

A. What idioms could you include in the paragraph? Write the idioms on the lines below. Remember, the idioms should express your ideas in a fun way.

1. _____   3. _____

2. _____   4. _____

B. Think of an Outstanding Opener for the paragraph.

_____

C. Now make a list of events to include in the paragraph.

1. _____   3. _____

2. _____   4. _____

D. Write a paragraph with the opener and events above, and the idioms that best express your ideas in a clever and interesting way.

_____

_____

_____

_____

Check Your Work

Are the idioms clever and interesting?

Whole Group Share your paragraph.

Add Personification to a Story

The wagon groaned as it started up the hill. The wagon is an object that is being described almost as though it is human. When the wagon made a noise, it was not groaning because wagons can't groan. However, the author described it as a groan. This is called personification. It is a type of figurative language. Writers can use personification to describe things in more vivid, exciting ways.

Whole Group As a group, practice finding and using personification.

A. Find the examples of personification below. Underline the object or animal that is being personified in each paragraph. Then circle the personification.

1. **The pink sock whirled and somersaulted in the clothes dryer until, finally, it found a towel to cling to.**

2. **Tom's bike's brakes squealed as the boy edged closer to the steel drop-off. When he bumped the pedals, they spun backward and chattered anxiously.**

3. **The excited player watched as the soccer ball jumped into the net to score the winning goal.**

B. Write human characteristics for the animals or objects below.

Animal or Object	**Human Characteristics**
1. **a car:**	_____
2. **a computer:**	_____
3. **the Sun:**	_____

Independently Write human characteristics for a cell phone. Then using personification, write a sentence using those human characteristics. Make the sentence fun to read.

Human Characteristics: _____

_____

Sentence: _____

_____

Whole Group Share the sentence about the cell phone.

Add Personification to a Story

Personification is when an animal or object is described with human characteristics. Personification is a type of figurative language. Writers can use personification to describe things in more vivid, exciting ways.

Personification Words

Verbs

chatter	hop	groan
squeal	sit	smile
wave	nod	cry

Adverbs

anxiously	sadly	frantically
joyfully	sleepily	confusedly
excitedly	wisely	fondly

Whole Group Let's prepare to write a paragraph using personification. The paragraph will be about a flower. Is the flower wilting? Is someone picking it?

A. Write human characteristics and actions that could describe the flower. Use the words from the box for help, or use any other words you can think of.

1. _____   3. _____

2. _____   4. _____

B. Think of an Outstanding Opener for the paragraph.

_____

C. Make a list of events and details to include in the paragraph. The events should be written in the order they will appear in the story.

1. _____   3. _____

2. _____   4. _____

Independently Now write the paragraph about the flower. Include the Outstanding Opener and events above. Include at least two human characteristics from Part A.

_____

_____

_____

_____

_____

Check Your Work

Is the paragraph entertaining?

Whole Group Share your paragraph.

Add Personification to a Story

Personification is describing an object or animal with human characteristics.

Anthropomorphism is making objects or animals the main characters in a story and having them act like people. Have you ever seen a movie or play in which the main characters were objects or animals? Did they talk and do other human things? This is anthropomorphism, and it is similar to personification.

Personification Example	**Anthropomorphism Example**
The tree's branches seemed to wave a greeting as the wind gusted through them.	*As I strolled by the old apple tree, it raised its arms and waved hello to me.*

Anthropomorphism Actions

having a party	playing a sport	watching a parade	shopping
living in a house	having a job	going on a quest	arguing

Partners   What happens in your classroom when you go home? What if the objects in your classroom came alive? With your partner, write about a desk talking to a chair.

A. Use anthropomorphism to make the desk and chair act like people. What human things could they do? Use the human actions from the list or any actions of your choice.

1. _____   3. _____

2. _____   4. _____

B. Write an Outstanding Opener.

_____

C. Now make a list of events to include in the paragraph.

1. _____   3. _____

2. _____   4. _____

D. Use anthropomorphism to write a paragraph about the desk and the chair. Include the information and anthropomorphism actions above. Use vivid and lively details.

_____

_____

_____

Check Your Work

What was the funniest part of the paragraph?

Whole Group Share your paragraph.

Add Personification to a Story

Personification is when an animal or object is described with human characteristics. Personification is a type of figurative language. Writers can use personification to describe things in more vivid, exciting ways.

Personification Words

Verbs			Adverbs		
chatter	hop	groan	anxiously	sadly	frantically
squeal	sit	smile	joyfully	sleepily	confusedly
wave	nod	cry	excitedly	wisely	fondly

Independently What human characteristics could a tree have? Can you describe a tree's branches to show how they are like arms? Could the leaves be like hands? An author could use personification to describe the tree more vividly.

A. Use personification and your imagination to make the ordinary objects below show human characteristics such as the ones listed in the box above.

Example

a window: *The window winked at me in the sunlight.*

1. **a house:** _____

2. **a skateboard:** _____

3. **a cloud:** _____

4. **a spider:** _____

B. Choose one or more of the sentences in Part A to include in a paragraph. The sentences can be written anywhere in the paragraph. Remember to begin the paragraph with an Outstanding Opener.

_____

_____

_____

_____

Check Your Work

Did personification emphasize the object in the paragraph?

Whole Group Share your paragraph.

Add Personification to a Story

Personification is when an animal or object is described with human characteristics. Writers can use personification to describe things in more vivid, exciting ways.

Personification Words

Verbs

chatter	hop	groan
squeal	sit	smile
wave	nod	cry

Adverbs

anxiously	sadly	frantically
joyfully	sleepily	confusedly
excitedly	wisely	fondly

Story Ideas

a kite getting caught in a tree   a plant blooming

a thunderstorm beginning   a log floating down a river

Independently Write a paragraph using personification.

A. Think of a story idea or choose one from the box above. Write it on the line.

_____

B. Write your own personification ideas for the characters. Use the box above for help.

1. _____   3. _____

2. _____   4. _____

C. Write an Outstanding Opener.

_____

D. Now make a list of events to include in the paragraph.

1. _____   3. _____

2. _____   4. _____

E. Write a paragraph using the information and personification ideas above.

_____

_____

_____

Check Your Work

Did the personification make the descriptions more vivid?

Whole Group Share your paragraph.

Five-Story Writing Checklist

It is time for you to use all the writing strategies you have learned. You will write five different stories. If you need an idea for a story, look at the Story Ideas on page 107. You must use a different Outstanding Opener and Fantastic Finale for each story. Include as many Terrific Transitions, Awesome Adjectives, and Fabulous Figurative Language strategies as needed to make a great story. Each story will take several days to complete, ending with a finished copy for your teacher to evaluate. Use this Five-Story Writing Checklist to check off the strategies you used to complete each of your stories.

	Story 1	Story 2	Story 3	Story 4	Story 5
Title					
Outstanding Openers					
Onomatopoeia					
Interrogative Sentences					
Dialogue					
Teasers					
Prepositional Phrases					
Terrific Transitions					
Beginning Transitions					
Continuing Transitions					
Ending Transitions					
Fantastic Finales					
Memories					
Decisions					
Wishes					
Feelings					
Interrogative Sentences					
Awesome Adjectives					
Physical Adjectives					
Sensory Adjectives					
Emotion Adjectives					
Personality Adjectives					
Fabulous Figurative Language					
Similes and Metaphors					
Idioms					
Personification					

Story Ideas

Can't think of an idea for a story? Try one of these.

You could write about . . .

having a nightmare

a special vacation

your grandparent

your life as a book

a trip to the moon

going on a hike

a sleepover

getting in trouble

going to the zoo

a special day at school

playing a sport

a talking giraffe

being a clown

winning a prize

planning a party for your dog

finding a treasure

a flower that won't stop growing

getting a new pet

winning a championship

breaking a promise

a strange creature

going on a picnic

being in a recital

a hurricane

your favorite holiday

meeting a movie star

your favorite movie

going to the mall

flying a kite

being the best at something

what you want to be someday

having your picture in the newspaper

babysitting a younger child

inventing a homework machine

being the teacher for a day

driving a car

a marathon

playing a musical instrument

decorating your bedroom

going skating

going on a roller coaster

being able to fly like a bird

_____

_____

_____

_____

_____

_____

_____

_____

_____

_____

Begin a Story with Onomatopoeia

Day 1, Page 6

Whole Group

Possible answers include:

1. Screech
2. Gurgle
3. Zoom / Whoosh
4. Thud
5. Sizzle

Independently

Words and sentences will vary.

Day 2, Page 7

Sentences and paragraphs will vary.

Day 3, Page 8

Partners / Independently

Possible answers include:

1. Screech / Whoosh / Ding
2. clang / bang / kurplunk
3. Click / Squeak / Whizz
4. clack / whizz / squeak
5. Ahhh / Squeak / Screech
6. zoomed / whizzed / whooshed
7. Whoosh / Zoom / Ahhh
8. Bang / Thud / Crash
9. rumbled / screeched / thudded

Day 4, Page 9

Sentences and paragraphs will vary.

Day 5, Page 10

Paragraphs will vary.

Begin a Story with an Interrogative Sentence

Day 1, Page 11

Whole Group

Possible answers include:

1. When does the movie start?
2. Where is the book?
3. Where is Paul? /
   Why did Paul leave class?

Independently

A — Possible answers include:

1. What was that noise outside? / Where was the kitten?
2. Where did Wanda find the article? / What work did Wanda do on the computer?
3. Where did Tiffany go with her mother? / How did Tiffany get to the mall?
4. Where did the boys meet? / Where did the boys play baseball?

B — Sentences will vary.

Day 2, Page 12

Sentences and paragraphs will vary.

Day 3, Page 13

Questions, answers, and paragraphs will vary.

Day 4, Page 14

Sentences and paragraphs will vary.

Day 5, Page 15

Paragraphs will vary.

Begin a Story with Dialogue

Days 1–5, Pages 16–20

Dialogues and paragraphs will vary.

Begin a Story with a Teaser

Day 1, Page 21

Whole Group

A

1. He woke up to find himself on a moving train.
2. I was eating my breakfast when suddenly the house became dark.
3. Something was on his pillow.

B — Teasers will vary.

Independently

Teasers will vary.

Day 2, Page 22

Paragraphs will vary.

Day 3, Page 23

Mysteries will vary.

Day 4, Page 24

Teasers and paragraphs will vary.

Day 5, Page 25

Paragraphs will vary.

Begin a Story with a Prepositional Phrase

Day 1, Page 26

Whole Group

A — Possible answers include:

1. On the wall, / Across the street,
2. Before school, / On Tuesday,
3. By the fireplace, / In her sleeping bag,
4. During lunch, / At the party,
5. On the field, / After school,

Sentences will vary.

Day 2, Page 27

Phrases and paragraphs will vary.

Day 3, Page 28

Partners

Circled phrases:

1. in my neighborhood
2. beyond the front gate
3. in her garden
4. against the back fence
5. along the crooked fence
6. during the evening
7. at the flowers
8. through the sprinklers

Sentences will vary.

Day 4, Page 29

Paragraphs will vary.

Day 5, Page 30

Paragraphs will vary.

Add Transitions to Connect Beginning Ideas

Day 1, Page 31

Whole Group

Possible answers include:

1. First / To start with
2. Earlier; just as
3. In the beginning, so that

Independently

Possible answers include:

1. Currently; For that reason
2. Before; Now
3. As soon as

Day 2, Page 32

Paragraphs will vary.

Day 3, Page 33

Sentences will vary.

Day 4, Page 34

Paragraphs will vary.

Day 5, Page 35

Paragraphs will vary.

Add Transitions to Continue Ideas

Day 1, Page 36

Whole Group

Possible answers include:

1. although / even though
2. For example / Afterward
3. Then / Eventually

Independently

Possible answers include:

1. However
2. even though
3. Usually

Day 2, Page 37

Paragraphs will vary.

Day 3, Page 38

Possible answers include:

"Yuck! My hair looks awful!" I complained. **Earlier,** I had told the barber to take a little off, not make me bald. Why don't people listen to me?

I should have known that it was going to be one of those days. **First,** my little sister took my favorite video game. **Then,** she tried to flush it down the toilet. I screamed at her. **Later,** my mom yelled at me for yelling at her, **but** Mom did not want to hear my side of the story.

Meanwhile, my dog, Dexter, knocked over his dish of food. **Afterward,** I had to clean it up. Dexter kept barking at me the entire time I was picking up his food. **Also,** he tried to bite me. He thought I was stealing it.

Day 4, Page 39

Paragraphs will vary.

Day 5, Page 40

Paragraphs will vary.

Add Transitions to End a Story

Day 1, Page 41

Whole Group

Possible answers include:

1. In the end
2. For this reason
3. Most importantly

Independently

Possible answers include:

1. for this reason
2. Basically
3. as a result

Day 2, Page 42

Sentences and paragraphs will vary.

Day 3, Page 43

Partners

Possible answers include:

1. First,
2. then
3. Now
4. To begin with,
5. after
6. especially
7. Most importantly,
8. Finally,
9. Therefore,

How-to essays will vary.

Day 4, Page 44

Sentences and paragraphs will vary.

Day 5, Page 45

Paragraphs will vary .

Close a Story with a Memory

Days 1–5, Pages 46–50

Sentences, logs, and paragraphs will vary.

Close a Story with a Decision

Days 1–5, Pages 51–55

Sentences, decisions, and paragraphs will vary.

Close a Story with a Wish

Days 1–5, Pages 56–60

Sentences, goals, and paragraphs will vary.

Close a Story with a Feeling

Days 1–5, Pages 61–65

Sentences, poems, and paragraphs will vary.

Close a Story with an Interrogative Sentence

Days 1–5, Page 66–70

Sentences, questions and answers, and paragraphs will vary.

Describe Appearances

Day 1, Page 71

Whole Group

Possible answers include:

1. tall; strong
2. young; powerful
3. tiny; sickly
4. clumsy; slim
5. huge; graceful

Independently

Nouns, adjectives, and sentences will vary.

Day 2, Page 72

Paragraphs will vary.

Day 3, Page 73

Word Search

Paragraphs will vary.

Day 4, Page 74

Adjectives and paragraphs will vary.

Day 5, Page 75

Paragraphs will vary.

Describe Details
Day 1, Page 76
Whole Group
Possible answers include:

1. red
2. furry
3. foul; fishy

Independently
Sentences will vary.

Day 2, Page 77
Nouns, adjectives, and paragraphs will vary.

Day 3, Page 78
Poems will vary.

Day 4, Page 79
Paragraphs will vary.

Day 5, Page 80
Paragraphs will vary.

Describe Feelings
Day 1, Page 81
Whole Group
Possible answers include:

1. annoyed; frustrated
2. concerned; frightened
3. cheerful; enthusiastic
4. excited; joyful
5. guilty; annoyed

Independently
Characters, adjectives, and sentences will vary.

Day 2, Page 82
Paragraphs will vary.

Day 3, Page 83
Partners

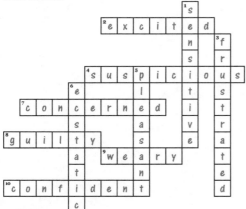

Independently
Paragraphs will vary.

Day 4, Page 84
Paragraphs will vary.

Day 5, Page 85
Paragraphs will vary.

Describe Characters
Day 1, Page 86

A — Possible answers include:

1. impatient; rude
2. motivated; intelligent
3. determined
4. creative; generous

Adjectives and sentences will vary.

Day 2, Page 87
Paragraphs will vary.

Day 3, Page 88
Partners

A–B
1. ambitious
2. cruel
3. creative
4. stubborn
5. impatient
6. conceited
7. optimistic
8. respectful

Paragraphs will vary.

Day 4, Page 89
Adjectives and paragraphs will vary.

Day 5, Page 90
Paragraphs will vary.

Add Similes and Metaphors to a Story
Day 1, Page 91
Whole Group

1. Devin was a rubber band when he was doing his gymnastic routine.
2. Our team had to stay as cool as a cucumber in order to win the basketball championship.
3. The lifeguard was a dolphin when he swam out to save the girl.

Independently

1. Debbie was as fresh as a daisy after her nap.
2. David's geography project was a train wreck.

Day 2, Page 92

Paragraphs will vary.

Day 3, Page 93

A

1. Molly heard the news and <u>roared like a lion</u>.
   Simile   Meaning: Molly yelled.
2. Carl <u>is like a snail</u> when he does his homework.
   Simile   Meaning: Carl works slowly.
3. My computer <u>is a dinosaur</u>.
   Metaphor   Meaning: My computer is very old.
4. His stomach <u>is a bottomless pit</u>.
   Metaphor   Meaning: His stomach is never full.

Similes, metaphors, and meanings will vary.

Day 4, Page 94

Paragraphs will vary.

Day 5, Page 95

Paragraphs will vary.

Add Idioms to a Story

Day 1, Page 96

Whole Group

1. back to square one
2. under the weather
3. it cost an arm and a leg
4. run out of steam

Independently

1. c
2. a
3. d
4. e
5. b

Day 2, Page 97

Paragraphs will vary.

Day 3, Page 98

Partners

1. To go to great lengths to try to please someone.
2. A situation where someone goes from being poor to being rich.
3. Something good that is added to another good thing.

Paragraphs will vary.

Day 4, Page 99

Paragraphs will vary.

Day 5, Page 100

Paragraphs will vary.

Add Personification to a Story

Day 1, Page 101

A

1. The <u>pink sock</u> (whirled and somersaulted) in the clothes dryer until, finally, (it found a towel to cling to.)
2. Tom's bike's <u>brakes</u> (squealed) as the boy edged closer to the steel drop-off. When he bumped the <u>pedals</u>, they (spun backward and chattered anxiously.)
3. The excited player watched as the <u>soccer ball</u> (jumped into the net to score the winning goal.)

Characteristics and sentences will vary.

Day 2, Page 102

Paragraphs will vary.

Day 3, Page 103

Paragraphs will vary.

Day 4, Page 104

Sentences and paragraphs will vary.

Day 5, Page 105

Paragraphs will vary.